COWBOY REUNIONS
of
LAS VEGAS
New Mexico

PAT ROMERO

A July 4, 1916, panoramic photograph of the participants, second Cowboys' Reunion, Cowboys' Park, Hot Springs Boulevard. The newly formed Cowboys' Reunion Band borrowed a drum from the Las Vegas Military Band. *Courtesy City of Las Vegas Museum and Rough Rider Memorial Collection, 97.10.1. Photo credit: Almeron Newman.*

Published by The History Press
Charleston, SC 29403
www.historypress.net

Copyright © 2012 by Pat Romero
All rights reserved

First published 2012

Manufactured in the United States

ISBN 978.1.60949.692.0

Library of Congress CIP data applied for.

Notice: The information in this book is true and complete to the best of our knowledge. It is offered without guarantee on the part of the author or The History Press. The author and The History Press disclaim all liability in connection with the use of this book.

All rights reserved. No part of this book may be reproduced or transmitted in any form whatsoever without prior written permission from the publisher except in the case of brief quotations embodied in critical articles and reviews.

For Biscotti, Neal, Domino, Jerry Lee, Sello, High Cotton, Rio, and all the other mounts who have joined those "Ghost Riders in the Sky"

"Las Vegas Reunion"
N. Howard "Jack" Thorp

Come on, all you cow-punchers,
To the round-up in July,
Where the Busters get together,
En the old broncs go sky-high;
We've got 'em spoiled en tricky,
Outlaws from far en near,
En we've got the boys to fork 'em
Who know not the word of fear.

The cry of all the cowboys now
Is "To the Meadow City or bust!"
From far Colorado's borders
They come a-spurrin' through the dust.
You don't see prairie-schooners
A-headin' now this way,
But 'mobiles come by thousands
To the Reunion's openin' day!

Cow-girls from far Montana
En the little Prairie Rose,
They can ride 'em slick en keerless
Es everybody knows;
So come on to the Meadow City,
The key's thrown plumb away,
En everybody's welcome
To the Cowboy's openin' day!

Chorus
With angora chaps en carnival hats,
Checked shirts en handkerchiefs loud,
Come straddle yer horse en ride with us,
Come ride with the Wild West crowd!
Fer we're jest cow-eatin' persons,
There's a welcome fer every one;
So whip up yer horse en lope across
To the Cowboys' Re-un-ion!

—Songs of the Cowboys
Courtesy of the University of Nebraska Press

Contents

Acknowledgements — 11
Introduction. More than a Rodeo — 13

Cowhand Context — 17
"Git Fer Vegas, Cowboy!" 1915 — 25
"A Sure Enough, All Around, Dyed-in-the-Wool, Successful
    Success," 1916–1931 — 37
"Let's Revive the Reunion," 1939–1951 — 57
"The Granddaddy of Them All," 1952–1968 — 73
The Las Vegas Cowboys' Reunion: A Retrospective — 87
The Git Fer Vegas, Cowboy! Exhibit — 93

Afterword — 97
Appendix I. Legends and Literati — 99
Appendix II. Cowboys' Reunion: A Chronology — 103
Appendix III. Selected Articles and Poetry — 107
Appendix IV. Cowhands and Rough Riders: What's the
    Connection? — 115
Sources — 119
Index — 123
About the Author — 128

Acknowledgements

Happily, this project received vital assistance from many generous people in Las Vegas, New Mexico, and from nearby ranches.

Thank you Linda Gegick, director of the City of Las Vegas Museum and Rough Rider Memorial Collection, for technical expertise, detective work, and encouragement.

Thank you to my excellent readers: Deb Blanche, Jane Hyatt, and Roy Luján.

Thank you Veronica C. Black for professionalism, exhibit photography, and video capture.

Thank you Deb Blanche for the verb "to neighbor," credited to Glen Rose of Somervell County, Texas.

Thank you Ismael Luján, Joe Luján, Roy Luján, Elsie Tapia, Eloy Garcia, Petey Salmon, George M. "Dogie" Jones, Pat Galligan, and Clyde Pickett for sharing Cowboys' Reunion recollections and New Mexico points of view.

Thank you Joe Lordi for enthusiasm and pep talks.

Thank you Martha McCaffrey, with the Citizens Committee for Historic Preservation, for your time and equipment.

At The History Press, thank you Jerry Roberts, commissioning editor, for guidance and a huge shoulder to cry on; Ryan Finn, project editor, for careful and thoughtful suggestions; and all staff members who worked on this project.

A special thank-you to Roy Luján for motivation and theoretical discussions.

Acknowledgements

Thank you Michael, Glenda, and Shannan Keenan for your Kansas perspectives.

My apologies to anyone I might have inadvertently left out. This book is not intended to be a comprehensive study but rather a first capture of important highlights and relevant issues and events surrounding the Cowboys' Reunions. Any shortcomings or misinterpretations are mine alone.

Introduction

MORE THAN A RODEO

Nearly every placita, jerkwater village, town and city in New Mexico has a rodeo. The one and only Cowboys' Reunion is in Las Vegas.
—*Audrey Simpson*

The Cowboys' Reunion events spanned five decades, and during that time, what was referred to as Las Vegas was actually two separate municipalities with separate governing bodies. However, most of the writing about the reunion events and publications of the times spoke of the area as one city: Las Vegas or, sometimes, Greater Las Vegas. From 1895 to 1970, Las Vegas was composed of two communities, each with its own complex history.

The current city, Las Vegas, dates its beginning as a settlement to the 1835 Mexican land grant. Originally named *Nuestra Señora de los Dolores de Las Vegas*, the community lay west of the Gallinas River and grew outward from a central plaza. According to Lynn I. Perrigo, in *Gateway to Glorieta*, this subsistence economy based on agriculture and sheep raising barely had a chance to develop before it was invaded by the United States in 1846 and inundated with new people and trade because of its proximity to the Santa Fe Trail (circa 1821–80) and Fort Union (1851–91). The village, nestled at the foot of the Sangre de Cristo Mountains and nourished by the Gallinas River, swelled with immigrants, traders, freighters, soldiers, speculators, and outlaws. In 1879, when the Atchison, Topeka & Santa Fe Railway (AT&SF) made a depot a few miles east of the plaza, it brought increased prosperity and a new town.

Introduction

Panoramic view of Las Vegas, circa 1910, from east of the Atchison, Topeka & Santa Fe Railway line. *Courtesy City of Las Vegas Museum and Rough Rider Memorial Collection, 2012.2.18.*

After the 1884 New Mexico territorial government disincorporated all municipalities that did not adhere to its new codes, the east side of the community, which came to be known officially as the City of Las Vegas, sometimes referred to as East Las Vegas, began reincorporation efforts that were ultimately realized in 1895 when the population reached the required three thousand. Meanwhile, until it reincorporated officially as the Town of Las Vegas in 1903, the west side continued to be operated under the San Miguel County government. The boundary between the two municipalities was marked primarily by the Gallinas River. Unless otherwise specified, in this work, the terms "Las Vegas" or "Greater Las Vegas" refer to the geographic and political areas that made up both communities between the years 1915 and 1968. The original founders of the Cowboys' Reunion and the Cowboys' Reunion Association hailed from both sides of the river.

At an elevation of 6,414 feet, Las Vegas, New Mexico, is located sixty miles northeast of Santa Fe on the edge of the eastern plains. Its climate is high desert. Although mostly dry and sunny, the area enjoys four seasons. Winter snows and monsoon rains feed the nearby watershed, but the area is subject to periodic drought conditions. Many large cattle and horse ranches, as well as several small communities, surround the city. Throughout the years since the beginnings of the Cowboys' Reunion, Las Vegas has experienced an interesting and eclectic collection of architectural periods, its buildings reflecting the early adobe styles, the prosperous 1880s and 1890s railroad boom period, and twentieth-century influences. The population, since the Santa Fe Trail, Fort Union, and the ATS&F days, remains multiethnic and multicultural.

In spite of its commercial heritage, the roots of Las Vegas were and are deep in its terra firma. Agriculture, sheep raising, and cattle ranching shaped its primary identity. However, these endeavors depend on many

Introduction

unpredictable variables, and Las Vegas periodically suffers financial recessions, unstable population figures, and climatic reversals such as drought and dust storms. Furthermore, as the territory grew into a state, the commercial and industrial centers shifted. As Perrigo points out, the Las Vegas social and commercial organizations of the 1890s searched for ways to strengthen the economy. Ultimately, one of those ventures, the New Mexico Cowboys' Reunion, took hold and "gave the local economy a shot in the arm for a few days seasonally."

The *Las Vegas Leading Industries and Business Enterprises* directory of 1915 notes that Las Vegas was "the third city in population" in the young state, and as the San Miguel county seat, it was considered a "clean, healthful, progressive city," a likely place to begin a new enterprise. The Cowboys' Reunion represented a new enterprise that reflected the major occupations of the area. From its beginning, the annual Cowboys' Reunion event was both a reunion and rodeo by and for working cowhands, ranchers, stockmen, rural families, and the community. More than a commercial venture and more than a rodeo, the annual Cowboys' Reunion at Las Vegas was a three- and sometimes four-day event including banquets, barbecues, balls, musical entertainment, parades, carnivals, fireworks, pie-eating contests, and cakewalks, as well as a highly respected "square-deal" rodeo. The reunions drew working cowhands, celebrity performers, exhibition acts, and huge crowds, as well as artists, poets, writers, popular dance bands, and songwriters.

By the time the Cowboys' Reunion came along, American rodeo was evolving from sharing skills at the end of a cattle drive to contests performed in front of spectators. And the Cowboys' Reunion rodeo grew to meet the demands of the new sport. The reunion at Las Vegas was part roundup, part Wild West show, part celebration of the ranching life, part "re-unionizing," and part community boosterism.

The New Mexico Cowboys' Reunion, as it was billed in its first year, was held annually from 1915 to 1931 and again from 1939 to 1967. The reunion

Introduction

and rodeo was one of the largest and better-known of the regional gatherings. Although it changed venues, managers, missions, titles, and perspectives throughout the years, the Cowboys' Reunion at Las Vegas offered rural families and neighbors the chance to get together and get reacquainted. The rodeo alone drew thousands of spectators, working and professional cowgirls and cowboys, contract and exhibition performers, championship competitors, celebrities, politicians, the western literati, and, of course, excellent horses and stock. Although there is no doubt that the annual reunion and rodeo provided a hefty "shot in the arm" to the community's economy, in reality, the event became a source of identity and pride.

As Walter Vivian put it, "Vegas without the Reunion just simply wouldn't be Vegas."

Cowhand Context

It was here that we held the <u>rodeo</u> that year [1886], *an unusually dry spring. A* rodeo *in those days truly meant a cattle roundup, not a public exhibition.*
—Fabiola Cabeza de Baca

Although it was created by and for working ranch cowhands of the Las Vegas area, the New Mexico Cowboys' Reunion was part of a longstanding tradition whose roots reached back as far as the idea of raising herd animals; as early as the seventeenth century, Pérez de Villagrá observed *vaqueros* and rodeos in *Nuevo México*. Today, as in 1915, the northern New Mexico ranching and farming culture is one of homesteads and ranches separated by thousands of acres of fenced grazing land and served by intermittent villages and small towns with a few gathering spots like the post office, a café, a bank, and a feed store. With vast distances and limited transportation separating neighbors, gatherings are special. "Neighboring" offers opportunities for people to get reacquainted; to share experiences, joys, and knowledge; and to offer one another support in times of need. Sometimes, neighboring opportunities, like the Cowboys' Reunion, had to be created.

Kristine Fredriksson, in *American Rodeo from Buffalo Bill to Big Business*, discusses the evolution of rodeo from end-of-the-trail roundup to the professional, athletic sport of the twenty-first century. She points out that the middle to the late nineteenth century saw the rise of a variety of planned gatherings intended specifically for rancher-cowhands throughout

A primary responsibility of the cowhand: rounding up the mavericks. *Courtesy City of Las Vegas Museum and Rough Rider Memorial Collection, 2011.2.815.*

the United States and Canada. Early gatherings grew out of informal cowhand contests at the end of a day's ranch work or a long cattle drive.

On the open range, when cowhands from different cattle outfits encountered one another, they often shared skills, engaged in contests and got caught up on the news and gossip. These gatherings represented a natural conclusion to the drive and, according to Fredriksson, often took place "in the town square of the railhead at the end of the cattle drive." Contest events usually included bronc riding and steer roping, but the gatherings were also reunions. Generally, there was lots of dancing, eating, drinking, and entertainment in celebration of a hard job well done.

Sometimes, cowhand gatherings took place within one cattle outfit, with contests held between the cattle-driving cowhands and the "reps" (riders hired specifically to round up strays). These riders brought their own string of wild horses, trained them on the range and then rode them to round up the mavericks. Another way the early contests happened was when large cattle operations or ranches hosted a rodeo competition among several different outfits, like today's ranch rodeos. Out of these spontaneous gatherings and contests grew the "public exhibitions," rodeos put on for paying spectators.

As Fredriksson puts it, "What was to become rodeo, as we know it today, was the play of the working cowboy, in which he would indulge during rare breaks…or when work was finished." As audiences were added to the mix, the "play of the working cowboy" developed into public exhibitions, Wild West spectacles, and, ultimately, the professional sport of rodeo.

Sometime after the Civil War, and fueled by journalists, Americans became fascinated with the outlaws and cowboys of the western frontier, and often there was little distinction between the two. The first recognized public cowhand competition in front of an audience occurred in Prescott, Arizona, on July 4, 1864, but it wasn't until 1888 that Prescott began charging admission, initiating the idea of cowboy contests as spectator sport.

Throughout the 1880s, as the days of open ranges dwindled, cowboying became seasonal work. At the same time, though, the daily activities of cowboys and cowgirls continued to interest the general public. Out of the early cowboy gatherings and the later development of charging admission grew the extravaganzas like Buffalo Bill's Wild West Show and Pawnee Bill's Wild West. William F. Cody, best known as "Buffalo Bill," first presented his big show on July 4, 1882, in his hometown of North Platte, Nebraska. These traveling spectacles, as well as more localized shows, provided venues in which "such a character as the rodeo cowboy" came into being, but this "character" represented a romanticized version of the daily work of cowgirls and cowboys.

The Wild West exhibitions threw together a conglomeration of staged western frontier scenes enacted to thrill and excite audiences. There was more shooting, wild riding, and outrageous costumes than actual reenactments, but the big shows included some cowboy and cowgirl events like saddle bronc riding, trick roping, steer roping, and trick riding. In 1885, about fifty Wild West shows were touring the United States. However unrealistic they may have been, the shows provided much-needed off-season employment for working cowhands.

In 1887, one journalist, John Baumann, developed the idea of "the cowboy myth." Baumann saw and perpetuated "all manner of romantic qualities" in cowboys, and according to Fredriksson, he possibly obscured the "true character of the cowboy." The myth hid the working cowhand's qualities behind "fantastic tales of impossible daring and skill of dare devil equitation and unexampled endurance. Every member of his class is pictured as a kind of Buffalo Bill." The myth was so hard to live up to that by 1892, an article in *Harper's Weekly* by Julian Ralph predicted the end of the "cowboy."

However, instead of bringing about the end of the cowboy, by the 1890s, journalists and, consequently, the American reading public had turned their attentions to the "working cowboy." The real job of a cowhand was soon recognized as "an occupation that required certain very special qualifications and one that did not attract just any wild and reckless man" or woman. This perception of cowhands stressed the qualities and skills needed to get the job done, such as a strong physical constitution, "an active mind," "steady nerve," and "fearless spirit." These skills, personal characteristics, and "sportsmanlike instincts" became popular through the media, primarily in newspaper and magazine articles, and were soon applied not only to the working cowhand but also to rodeo cowboys and cowgirls.

In 1897, Cheyenne Frontier Days, billing itself as the "Daddy of 'Em All," began celebrating the "every-day" frontier experience. Similar shows like the Calgary (Canada) Exhibition and Stampede, the Pendleton (Oregon) Round Up, and the New Mexico Cowboys' Reunion came along a little later and celebrated the daily activities of ranching and farming families, provided opportunities for getting together, and included up to four full days of rodeo contests. As the twentieth century dawned, interest in the western American experience continued to grow, and these frontier celebrations—part Wild West show and part neighboring—thrived.

Although they provided the venue and opportunities for seasonal work for cowhands, both the big shows and some of the smaller regional celebrations were often mismanaged. Big prizes, offered to draw in contestants, were not always awarded, and the term "championship" was overused and lost its validity. Contestants (cowhands needing work between roundups) were exploited. Consequently, by the beginning of the twentieth century, the contestants began seeing the promoters and managers as "a bad breed of people, not to be trusted." As early as 1916, Fay Ward, in the publication *The Wild Bunch*, discussed the need for unionization to protect and support rodeo contestants. At the same time, though, the gatherings and rodeos had a unifying effect on small ranching communities and often catered to the local working cowhand.

Into this ever-evolving rodeo arena entered the Cowboys' Reunion and its rodeo, from the start advertised in *The Wild Bunch* as a "square deal for all." In 1912, after a long, difficult struggle, New Mexico Territory became a state, and by the summer of 1915, the First Annual New Mexico Cowboys' Reunion was celebrated in Las Vegas on July 1–4. The event combined a working cowboy-rancher rodeo with a reunion of ranch and farm families, cowhands, stock producers, and Las Vegas "civilians." Reunion organizers were themselves ranchers and cowhands, and with the help of the local business folk, they put on a three-day shindig with a fancy ball, a monster parade, western "barbecue," two carnivals, and a rodeo that had to be extended to a fourth day to accommodate all contestants. Thousands of people from throughout the young state and beyond flocked to Las Vegas. They came by automobile over rutted dirt roads, in luxury trains, by wagon, and on horseback.

Throughout the ensuing years, the Cowboys' Reunion grew in popularity and earned a solid reputation for its "square deal for all." By the mid-1920s, the Las Vegas Cowboys' Band, begun in 1915, had grown to thirty-two musicians and was touring the United States, as well as performing a gig in London. World War I, the American stock market crash, and the Great Depression took their toll, and by 1932, the Cowboys' Reunion had closed its gates—down but not out.

In 1939, Leonard Hoskins Post No. 24 of the American Legion revived the great event and began the count all over again with the First Annual American Legion Cowboys' Reunion. As with the first phase, the revival included parades, dinners, dances, big-name entertainment, opportunities to gather and "neighbor," and a three-day rodeo. Although it renamed and renumbered the reunions, built a new park, and changed the meeting days, the American Legion always included the name "Cowboys' Reunion" and billed the annual event as a "Revival of New Mexico's Most Famous Frontier Show!"

As it turned out, the revival reentered the rodeo world as it was taking a major turn on its way to professionalism and enjoying a renewed national popularity. Fredriksson believes that from the late 1940s to the mid-1950s was the "golden age of rodeo" and that with much public attention and publicity, rodeo soon attracted non-cowboys—that is, professional athletes who may never have worked on a ranch but who competed with working cowboys. This situation brought tension because of an unevenness in skills and attitudes and due to increased entry fees. Ultimately, on the national level, this tension led to new developments and specializations among rodeo contestants.

In Las Vegas, the Cowboys' Reunion rodeo felt the tension as it turned to professional production companies like Johnny Mullins, the Beutler Brothers Company, and Tommy Steiner. These rodeo producers put on flashy shows with well-turned-out riders and horses. Additionally, increased prize

"Rodeo" means roundup. Identified as "Union Land and Grazing," northwest of Las Vegas. *Courtesy City of Las Vegas Museum and Rough Rider Memorial Collection, 2009.27.52. Photographer: Maurice Eby.*

monies attracted professional and semiprofessional rodeo contestants from throughout the country. In 1952, the American Legion Cowboys' Reunion partnered up with the Roosevelt's Rough Rider Association, which had been enjoying its own annual reunions in various parts of the country since 1899. Each year from 1952 to 1967, Las Vegas and the Cowboys' Reunion honored the remaining members of the First United States Volunteer Cavalry, veterans of the Spanish-American War. Their presence increased attendance for both events.

Between the years 1915 and 1932 and the years 1939 and 1967, the people from both sides of the Gallinas River, big and small ranchers, local businesses, and civic organizations hosted a gathering of "Cowboys, Cowgirls, and Humans" that was both rodeo and reunion. Throughout the years, the Cowboys' Reunion attracted working cowhands, as well as professional contestants, top-notch stock, exhibition acts, and soon-to-be-famous western literati and celebrities.

The first phase of the reunion at Las Vegas hosted big names like Tom Mix, "Tex" Austin, "Idaho Bill" Pearson, N. Howard "Jack" Thorp, Randall Davey, Ruth Monro Augur, Prairie Rose Henderson, Montana Belle, and Will

Identified as the First Cowboys' Reunion, lining up for a photo shoot. *Courtesy George M. "Dogie" Jones Private Collection.*

James in addition to the cream of the working cowboy and cowgirl crop from throughout the Midwest and Southwest. The American Legion phase drew rodeo producers, champion cowhands like Jim Shoulders, major attractions like the Rough Riders, and celebrity activities such as the *Queen for a Day* television show. In addition, artists Edward Borein and M.J. Davis, writer S. Omar Barker, and popular musicians trekked to Las Vegas for the annual doings.

Although it changed names, slogans, sponsors, venues, dates, and objectives, the New Mexico Cowboys' Reunion at Las Vegas persevered through wars, national and regional financial ups and downs, natural disasters, social unrest, and major upheavals to American mores and values. For close to five generations, the Cowboys' Reunion was, in the words of S. Omar Barker, "a ripsnorting contest and a real ranch-folks Reunion."

Whether it was pure *rodeo* like the cattle roundups, a public exhibition of cowhand skills and braggadocio, or a commercial venture is a question this book aims to explore. More than likely, the Cowboys' Reunion was a hybrid—crossing the wild prairie mustang with the domesticated, and sometimes not-so-domesticated, working and bucking equine.

"Git Fer Vegas, Cowboy!"
1915

The organization was therefore incorporated to be known as the "Cowboys' Reunion Association"…the Cowboys at large to own and control the affairs at all times.
—*Cowboys' Reunion Association letter*

Some say that the Cowboys' Reunion at Las Vegas began as a lark, a bit of "western" entertainment for the eastern visitors. Another popular version of how "New Mexico's biggest ranch-folks get-together" got together is that Tom Mix arrived and showed Las Vegas how to put on a "cowboy contest." Other accounts name the Cowboys' Reunion as the "offspring of the Roosevelt's Rough Rider Reunion encampment of 1899."

In *Gateway to Glorieta*, Lynn I. Perrigo states that sometime around 1915, the Las Vegas Commercial Club, a community and business booster organization, proposed "a cowboy roundup" to amuse and astonish summer visitors and Normal College students. Perrigo also connects the first Cowboys' Reunion of 1915 to the 1899 Rough Rider Reunion and the 1905 Northern New Mexico Fair, both of which took place in Las Vegas and included rodeo events.

Much local lore spread the idea that the Cowboys' Reunion was the "offspring" of the first Rough Rider Reunion of 1899 and that even when there was not a rodeo happening, cowboys gathered in Las Vegas for informal competitions. The Las Vegas area, from its early village days, was involved in raising, shipping, and trading herd animals. Consequently, cowhands and ranchers naturally would have gathered in Las Vegas, as it was a major railhead, "to rodeo" and swap stories, the core motivations for establishing the Cowboys' Reunion. As declared in *The Wild Bunch*, "The Reunion boys want their show, besides being one of classy contests, one, also, of a real get-to-getherness. They want to hear the familiar 'howdy' of the boys who haven't seen each other in a coyote's age."

Although stories of a connection between the Rough Riders and the First Annual New Mexico Cowboys' Reunion of 1915 persist and carry with them a fine patina of tradition and pride, the relationship is tenuous. First, there is a span of sixteen years between the Rough Rider Encampment and the first Cowboys' Reunion. Second, there is no evidence of any Rough Riders being involved in organizing the Cowboys' Reunion. What seems the most likely story of the origins of the Cowboys' Reunion is the one the cowboys themselves told—the one involving the Las Vegas Commercial Club and the area ranchers, families, and cowhands who conceived of and put on that first event and then, in their words, "perfected" the Cowboys' Reunion Association.

The Las Vegas Commercial Club was an early and persistent organization that worked hard to develop a strong economic base for San Miguel County. Part of a national-level group, this local chapter pulled together resources, supported local enterprises, and developed land sales, irrigation projects, public health services, educational facilities, and tourism. Commercial Club literature claims that it grew out of the Montezuma Club, which had been an exclusive club for men of the business and banking communities. The Commercial Club was housed in the Masonic Lodge rooms on the second floor, formerly those occupied by the defunct Montezuma Club.

As early as 1892, the club produced *The Commercial Club Illustrated Supplement to the Las Vegas Daily Optic*, which describes the area, its history, commercial and agricultural endeavors, social clubs, educational systems, publishers, publications, recreational advantages, transportation, irrigation projects, and leading business citizens. The supplement states, "The Commercial Club is composed of the active and progressive business men of the city."

In 1915, the Commercial Club was featured in the thirty-one-page *Boost and Build Edition of the Las Vegas Daily Optic*, as well as the chapter "San Miguel County" by George A. Fleming in *New Mexico: The Land of Opportunity*, a 1915 national publication prepared for the Panama-California Exposition in San Diego, California. The Commercial Club advertisement announced, "An era of prosperity pervades Las Vegas; here health and wealth await you." As part of its commitment to Las Vegas, the Commercial Club worked closely with area ranchers to establish and produce the First Annual New Mexico Cowboys' Reunion; its secretary, Phil LeNoir, created the first slogan, "Git Fer Vegas, Cowboy!"

As news of what would become World War I trickled into the United States, Las Vegas hosted the first gathering of New Mexico "Cowboys, Cowgirls, and Humans." And right from the "git fer," the Cowboys' Reunion drew the attention of the wild and woolly rodeo crowd. Working cowgirls and cowboys, as well as celebrities, came from throughout New Mexico and neighboring states. Actor-director Tom Mix (1880–1940), who had moved with the Selig Polyscope Company to Las Vegas, participated in the first Cowboys' Reunion. Additionally, at the 1915 rodeo, the studio filmed scenes of *How Weary Went Wooing* and Mix portrayed Weary competing in a horse race. The film also includes a shot of the first Cowboys' Reunion poster. That first reunion rodeo brought Colonel William "Idaho Bill" Pearson and seventy-five of his wildest bucking horses. Pearson, a perennial favorite on the rodeo circuit, was a former Kit Carson scout. J.V. "Tex" Austin, who became famous for producing the New York and Chicago rodeos, got his boots dusty at the early reunion rodeos and was one of the founding members of the Cowboys' Reunion Association. World famous trick roper Johnny Judd and wild bull rider "Texas Annie" also showed up for the first big roundup.

The *Las Vegas Daily Optic* (or just the *Optic*) provided both advanced notices and follow-up reports. The parade—more like a pageant—kicked off the event on Thursday, July 1, as it crisscrossed the Gallinas River and "featured Las Vegas Day, the opening day of the First Annual Reunion of the Cowboys of New Mexico." Local rancher Walter A. Naylor, described in the *Optic* as "a tall, rather angular man," served as parade marshal, followed by the Las Vegas Military Band, a string of seventy-five wild horses, "cowboys galore, in ranks of four," two chuck wagons, and various parade floats. The E. Romero Hose and Fire Company float took first prize, Bacharach Brothers second, and the Las Vegas Roller Mill third. Local stores and banks closed at noon to allow folks to attend the festivities, and spectators, dressed in western-style boots, blue jeans, plaid shirts, and cowboy hats, lined the streets.

Parade participants gathered in the fields at the north end of Sixth Street, proceeded south on Sixth Street to Douglas Avenue, went "around the loop" at the triangle of Grand Avenue and Sixth Street (at that time the Clement Block), returned to Douglas, traveled west and then dispersed at the Old Town Plaza Park. The rodeo competitors turned right and rode north on Hot Springs Boulevard to "Gallinas Park." The float judges—Mrs. W.E. Gortner, Mrs. Frank H.H. Roberts, Dr. M.F. Des Marais, Mayor H.M. Smith and Colbert C. Root—were positioned at the Crockett Building on the corner of Sixth Street and Douglas Avenue.

First Cowboys' Reunion parade, 1915, Douglas Avenue. *Courtesy City of Las Vegas Museum and Rough Rider Memorial Collection, 76.4.10.*

Previous, bottom: The Loop, 1903. Early reunion parades followed a route that included a loop around the Clement Building at the triangle of Sixth Street and Grand Avenue, then back to Douglas Avenue and west to the town plaza. *Courtesy City of Las Vegas Museum and Rough Rider Memorial Collection, 2009.27.6. Photo credit: Fred Geyer.*

Rodeo activities took place at Gallinas Park, which Perrigo, in *Gateway to Glorieta*, also refers to as "the former fairgrounds." According to Perrigo, twelve years before the reunion of 1915, the Las Vegas Driving Park and Fair Association, led by Charles Ward, Robert Taupert, and Ralph Emerson Twitchell, had raised funds and built a driving park. That park opened in 1903 "on the flats west of the [Gallinas] river near where the car track bridged that river, about three miles north of town." Based on Sandborn Insurance Company maps and the description in *Las Vegas Gallinas Park and the Scenic Highway*, the car track that "bridged" the river would have been the Las Vegas Electric Trolley, which at that time ran from the ATS&F Depot on Railroad Avenue west across town and north on Hot Springs Boulevard for about one mile beyond the then town limits. The Hot Springs Branch of the AT&SF Railway ran west from the depot and turned north along the east side of the Gallinas River to Las Vegas Hot Springs, later named Montezuma. So, the park must have been on the river bottom lands bordered on the east by the river and the railroad tracks and on the west by Hot Springs Boulevard and the trolley tracks. According to the *Optic*, the Santa Fe Railroad provided transport to and from Gallinas Park for the rodeo activities with service on the half-hour from 11:30 a.m. to 2:30 p.m.

The promotional booklet *Las Vegas Gallinas Park and the Scenic Highway* provides photographs and describes the area. The park included carriage driving boulevards, a racecourse, stables, a grandstand, an athletic field, a pure water supply, and electric power and lights. Intended for resting and training horses, the park sporadically hosted rodeos, horse races, Indian dances, and a variety of athletic competitions, including baseball games. Although an excellent site for reunion activities, the park suffered damage from a flood and was rebuilt but had not been in regular use. By 1915, it may have been in need of repair.

In an article entitled "Git Fer Vegas, Cowboy!" published in *Frontier Times*, S. Omar Barker described the park as it was used for the Cowboys' Reunion rodeos. He mentions corrals, a half-mile racetrack, an arena, and a grandstand "but no chutes." Barker explains how things worked:

> *Critters were turned out through a hand-operated gate in a corral fence. There was no loudspeaker except the announcer's own bellow through a megaphone. Fog Horn Clancy got his nickname via megaphone. At Las Vegas it was usually the buzzsaw voice of an old cowhand named Brite Bagley that kept the crowd posted.*

According to the *Optic*, on the second day of the first reunion, adding to the thousands who had already arrived, thirty automobiles carrying over one

Cowboy Reunions of Las Vegas, New Mexico

Gallinas Park, circa 1904. At one time, the site of the Las Vegas Driving Park and Fair Association, the park included a racecourse, driveways, boulevards, and stable facilities. It was likely the site of the first reunion rodeo, 1915, and later Cowboys' Reunion Park. *Courtesy City of Las Vegas Museum and Rough Rider Memorial Collection, 87.2.1. Photo credit: J.A. Stirrat.*

Opposite, bottom: Dance card from the first Cowboys' Reunion Ball, July 2, 1915, Duncan Opera House, Las Vegas. Dances included quadrilles, waltzes, rags, *varsouvianas*, a Virginia reel, and a tango two-step. *Courtesy City of Las Vegas Museum and Rough Rider Memorial Collection, 73.16.4.*

hundred people came from Wagon Mound. State engineer James A. French brought "a large party of Capital City people," and state fair organizers from Albuquerque arrived.

Day two was barbecue day. Hundreds of people partook of the noontime meal and reunited at Gallinas Park on the riverbank for barbecued beef, buns, pickles, and coffee—"to many their first experience at a barbecue." The cooks' committee consisted of Walt Lynam, Hayward and C.C. Lewis, and George Sutherland, who also oversaw the big barbecues at Cheyenne Frontier Days.

That night, Friday, July 2, after a full day of activities and rodeo contests, everyone got spruced up and gathered at the Duncan Opera House at the corner of Sixth Street and Douglas Avenue for the First Annual Cowboys' Reunion Ball. Completed in 1886, the Duncan had many new features, like removable seats, allowing for either an entertainment venue or floor space for dancing. All were invited to trip the light fantastic with waltzes, polkas, rags, quadrilles, reels, and a *varsouviana*. But there was a condition. Printed at the bottom of each dance card are the words, "Cowboys only with their togs allowed to participate in the first 12 numbers."

First-year rodeo events listed in the daily newspaper insert included trick roping, steer riding, horse races, burro roping, a Ladies' Cowpony Race, a chuck

FIRST ANNUAL NEW MEXICO CO

PROGRAM INSERT
SATURDAY, JULY
GIVING REVISED RULES AND LIST O

EVENT NO. 1—Trick Roping, by Johnny Judd, world's champion trick roper.

EVENT NO. 2—Steer Riding.
Joe Ryan, 101.
Hill Burrow, 96.

EVENT NO. 3—Tournament Race.
Jim Whitmore, 80.
A. B. Bagley, 6.
F. W. Nations, 65.
Julian Sena, 89.
Gib George, 32.
W. E. Gillespie, 83.
Bill Davis, 20.
A. L. Beal, 8.
Salem Curtis, 13.

EVENT NO. 4—Horse Race, Free for All, 440 Yards.
Bert Auge, 102.
A. L. Clark, 14.
Chas. Burks, 11.
Ed. Gallegos, 33.
Secundino Romero, 68.
Ricardo Romero, 70.
Gib George, 32.
Tito Melendez, 55.
Earl Kelly, 49.
Manuel Valdez, 78.
S. L. Fisher, 30.
Lorenzo Delgado, 21.
A. L. Beal, 8.

EVENT NO. 5—Pack Race.
Bill Davis, 20.
Jose Romero, 69.
A. B. Bagley, 6.
Agapito Garcia, 35.
Salem Curtis, 13.
John Judd, 46.
Margarito Garcia, 34.
Jim Whitmore, 80.
Jack Curry, 90.

Joe Ryan, 101.
Jack Fretz, 29.
Clarence Woody, 81.
Sandy Fluitt, 28.

EVENT NO. 6—Burro Roping.
1st, $150; 2nd, $75; 3rd, $25.
(This is the rule under which this race will be run.)

Head or neck catch. No feet allowed in loop. Fine of fifteen seconds imposed for each foot in loop. Burro allowed 60 feet start. Each contestant must tie three feet with hogging string. Rider allowed to have loop made. Judges to pass on tie.

Vollie McKinney, 61.
Julian Sena, 89.
Bill Barnes, 9.
Lee Utterbach, 93.
Hill Burrow, 96.
Sandy Fluitt, 28.
F. W. Nation, 65.
Oscar Neafus, 62.
Sid Dennis, 87.
H. A. Wood, 94.

EVENT NO. 7—Ladies' Cowpony Race One-half Mile.
Catch entries at Paddock.

EVENT NO. 8—Chuck Wagon Race.
EVENT NO. 9—Potato Race.
PURSE $10—ONE MONEY
(This is the rule under which this race will be run.)

Two teams, four men each. Potatoes placed in center box. Each team's box to be one hundred feet from center box. Man to spear potatoes and put in his team's box. Each team allowed one guard over opponent's box. No potatoes to be knocked off stick within 10 feet of center box. Team

having most potatoes in end of three minutes v
Oscar Neafus' Team.
Geo. Bagley's Team.

EVENT NO. 10—Remour
A. B. Bagley, 6.
Jim Giles, 37.
Joe Ryan, 101.
Julian Sena, 89.
John Judd, 46.
Walter Lynam, 95.
Gib George, 32.
Lee Utterbach, 93.
S. L. Fisher, 30.
Fred Atkinson, 2.
Thad Pippin, 66.
E. Crossett, 19.
Will Davis, 20.
Agapito Garcia, 35.
Manuel Valdez, 78.
Jose Romero, 69.

EVENT NO. 11—Goat R
Clarence Woody, 81.
Margarito Garcia, 34.
Owen Woody, 91.
Agapita Garcia, 35.
Jose Romero, 69.
Jim Lovelady, 53.
Victor Eppes, 17.
Fred Atkinson, 2.
Sid Dennis, 87.
Jim Hobson, 41.
Tom Greer, 99.
Julian Sena, 89.
Lee Utterbach, 93.
Manual Valdez, 78.

wagon race, potato race, goat roping contest, a bareback cigar race, steer bulldogging, and bronc riding. Texas Annie riding a wild bull was listed as an exhibition act.

A story reported in Milton Callon's book *Las Vegas, New Mexico...The Town that Wouldn't Gamble* relates the tale of Tom Mix and the Selig Motion Picture Company's Daredevil Performers challenging the "Best Talent of the New Mexico Cowboys' Reunion" to a potato race. The program insert for July 4, 1915, lists these two gangs under event no. 5, the Stage Coach Race, and indicates that the teams were yet to be picked. But Charles O'Malley, eyewitness and longtime Reunion Rodeo supporter, told the story this way: "Our lads were enthusiastic but… they became confused over the idea of the race. They kept spearing the moving picture fellows." When the judges counted the spuds in each box, "the dad-burned dudes had out-scored the real he-man, gun-totin' hombres [by a score of] 18–11."

At the time, the potato race was a popular rodeo event, and it seems that this one was either added to the schedule or substituted for the chuck wagon race. By 1916, the potato race was a scheduled rodeo event, but these novelty races fell out of favor as rodeo became more and more professional. As Callon describes it, a potato race was a timed, team competition with four riders on each team "equipped with sticks which they

First New Mexico Cowboys' Reunion Rodeo Schedule. It was a great way to get the word out in 1915—a daily listing of events, contestants, and special exhibitions as inserts in newspapers. *Courtesy City of Las Vegas Museum and Rough Rider Memorial Collection, 73.16.8.*

The potato race. In 1915, Tom Mix's "dad-burned dudes" outscored the "real he-man, gun-toting' hombres." Postcard. *Courtesy City of Las Vegas Museum and Rough Rider Memorial Collection, 2000.16.8. Photographer: Almeron Newman.*

used to spear potatoes from a central box." Two teams took part in each race and tried to spear and deposit as many potatoes as possible in their home boxes. Each contestant galloped to the central box, impaled a potato, and dashed one hundred feet back to the home box. The team with the most spuds in its home box won the event.

THE COWBOYS' REUNION ASSOCIATION: "THE FIRST CONTEST ASSOCIATION OWNED AND OPERATED BY REAL HANDS AND COMMON COWBOYS EXCLUSIVELY"

The first reunion was deemed a financial success, prompting the organizers to "perfect" the Cowboys' Reunion Association (CRA). The *Optic* headlines proclaimed, "Cowboys Make Reunion Annual Event and Perfect a Permanent Organization—Naylor President." On July 3, before the arena dust settled, the organizers of the first reunion met and did indeed "Perfect a Permanent Organization."

A letter from William Springer to Walt Naylor on October 28, 1915, outlines the organization and lists the following founding members:

President Walter A. Naylor, Vice-President J.O. Neafus, Treasurer Donald Stewart, and Secretary William H. Springer. The first board members, in addition to the officers, were Secundino Romero, G.M. "Butch" Jones, J.V. "Tex" Austin, Walter Lynam, J.A. Wilson, J.A. Whitmore, A.B. Bagley, M.G. Keenan, and Apolonio A. Sena.

On July 21, 1915, E.E. Huyck, acting as agent for the new group, filed the corporation status as New Mexico Domestic Profit, and by October, the CRA was seeking shareholders at ten dollars per share, limited to a maximum of ten shares per shareholder. The organization made it clear that proceeds from the sale of stock shares would be dedicated to perpetuating the annual reunion—"by cowboys for cowboys."

In advertisements for its rodeo, the CRA proudly proclaimed "a square deal to [each] contestant if we don't make a dime!" reflecting the growing mistrust of regional managers among rodeo contestants. As reported in *The Wild Bunch*, the first year's Cowboys' Reunion rodeo saw 117 contestants, "and every one of these hands at the finish of the

Charter members of the first Cowboys' Reunion Association Board of Directors, Lincoln Park, Las Vegas, New Mexico, circa 1915: Jim Whitmore (second from left); Walter Naylor, president (fourth from left); G.M. "Butch" Jones (fifth from left); J.A. "Art" Wilson (sixth from left); and A.B. "Brite" Bagley (seventh from left). *Courtesy City of Las Vegas Museum and Rough Rider Memorial Collection, 76.3.2.*

Reunion agreed that they had had a fair square deal." In the report, the CRA stressed that there would be no false "champion of the world" belts. Instead, items would be engraved with specific details: "Winner such and such an event—Cowboys Reunion—Las Vegas, New Mexico, 1916."

In spite of awarding $2,842.50 in cash prize money, the first reunion earned a net gain after expenses of $1,087.68. Phil LeNoir, Cowboys' Reunion general chairman and Commercial Club secretary, proclaimed that "the 1915 Reunion stands as a sure enough, all around, dyed-in-the-wool successful Success." LeNoir had been a driving force behind the scenes, promoting and managing the big event. A writer of western fiction and poetry, he coined the first reunion slogan: "Git Fer Vegas, Cowboy!" LeNoir continued his enthusiastic support until his untimely death in 1923. Throughout the 1910s and 1920s, the CRA maintained a working relationship with the Commercial Club and held its official meetings in the club's rooms in the Masonic Lodge on Douglas Avenue.

To close out the year 1915, the Cowboys' Reunion Association held its First Annual Mid-Winter Ball at the armory building in Las Vegas on December 31. Based on the account in *The Wild Bunch*, it was also a "successful Success":

> *The cowboy dance at E. Las Vegas, was the biggest event of its kind ever pulled off in that town for some time. The big armory...was plumb filled and everyone danced until the rooster crowed in the morning sun. The place was decorated like an old '49 [1849] interior. There were the typical signs, the saddles, chaps, etc., and an imitation of the old time bar, but there being a large number of the fair sex present nothing stronger than spikeless punch was served.*

The Cowboys' Reunion filled a need for the two communities straddling the Gallinas River. It reunited the men and women of the nearby ranching and farming communities, brought visitors from throughout New Mexico and the Southwest, and provided an instantly recognizable identity for Las Vegas as the "Cowboy Capital of the Great Southwest."

"A Sure Enough, All Around, Dyed-in-the-Wool, Successful SUCCESS,"
1916–1931

Beginning with a parade, the like of which has never been seen in the southwest, the 1916 Las Vegas Cowboys' Reunion opened here on July 4th with a crowd that taxed the capacity of Las Vegas to the limit. The parade was over a mile long and in part consisted of 500 cowboys and cowgirls, one hundred trades floats, the G.A.R. and then a corp of Old Timers, men who rode the range thirty years ago.
—The Wild Bunch

Articles and advertisements about the Cowboys' Reunion were filled with hyperbole, from LeNoir's "successful SUCCESS" financial report to rodeo program claims of "the largest," "the biggest," and "the like of which has never been seen in the southwest." But the event's success was real. As the July 1, 1918 *Optic* reported, "contestants are arriving from all sections of the west in flivvers [automobiles], and rattlers. High boots and beaver hats are becoming more numerous in Las Vegas than they have been since the last gathering of the punchers." And that year, well-known announcer Fred "Foghorn" Clancy kept the spectators informed. For the following year, the fifth reunion, the *Optic* ran a story entitled, "1919 Reunion Broke Record for the Number of Visitors." Reunion attendance continued strong throughout the rest of the 1910s and into the national frenzy for good times called the Roaring Twenties. As reported in *The Wild Bunch* in 1916: "The first day at the park saw the largest crowd ever assembled in any enclosure in this part of the country. The Governor

Cowboy Reunions of Las Vegas, New Mexico

By the 1920s, the reunions were going strong, attracting working cowhands, trick riders and ropers, champion cowgirls and cowboys, rodeo promoters, clowns, and children. In 1924, the Las Vegas Cowboy Band toured internationally. All paraded through the streets of the two communities. Panoramic photograph of parade participants taken at the intersection of Grand Avenue and Lincoln Street. *Courtesy City of Las Vegas Museum and Rough Rider Memorial Collection, 70.7.4. Photo credit: Almeron Newman.*

[W.C. McDonald] dedicated the new park...and then the show was on. With a snap and a vim the events, under the direction of Texas Austin, the Arena Director, were pulled off in true professional style."

Contributing to the reunion successes were the rodeos; in fact, the two terms became synonymous. The new rodeo "plant," Cowboy Park, attracted both local and well-known contestants. However, the hard work of the ranchers, cowhands, and the people of the Las Vegas communities in organizing and promoting the entire reunion event ensured that everything went off as planned. In addition to CRA promotional activities, contestants and spectators spread the word about the good times in Vegas. The Cowboys' Reunion Band and its international tour with "Tex" Austin promoted the events, and a national fascination with the cowhand culture focused attention on the Las Vegas show. With each annual event, the Cowboys' Reunion rose in popularity among rodeo contestants and visitors in search of the "Wild West." Throughout the first phase of the Cowboys' Reunion, working ranch hands, movie cowboys, world-class trick riders and ropers, bronc-busting cowgirls, and professional rodeo promoters, as well as poets, artists, storytellers, and songwriters, annually descended on Las Vegas to celebrate what CRA programs referred to as the "First Contest Association Owned and Operated by Real Hands and Common Cowboys Exclusively."

Based on accounts in the *Optic*, after the success of the first reunion, the CRA purchased Gallinas Park and rebuilt the facilities to suit rodeo needs. It became known as Cowboys' Park. Just in time for the second Cowboys'

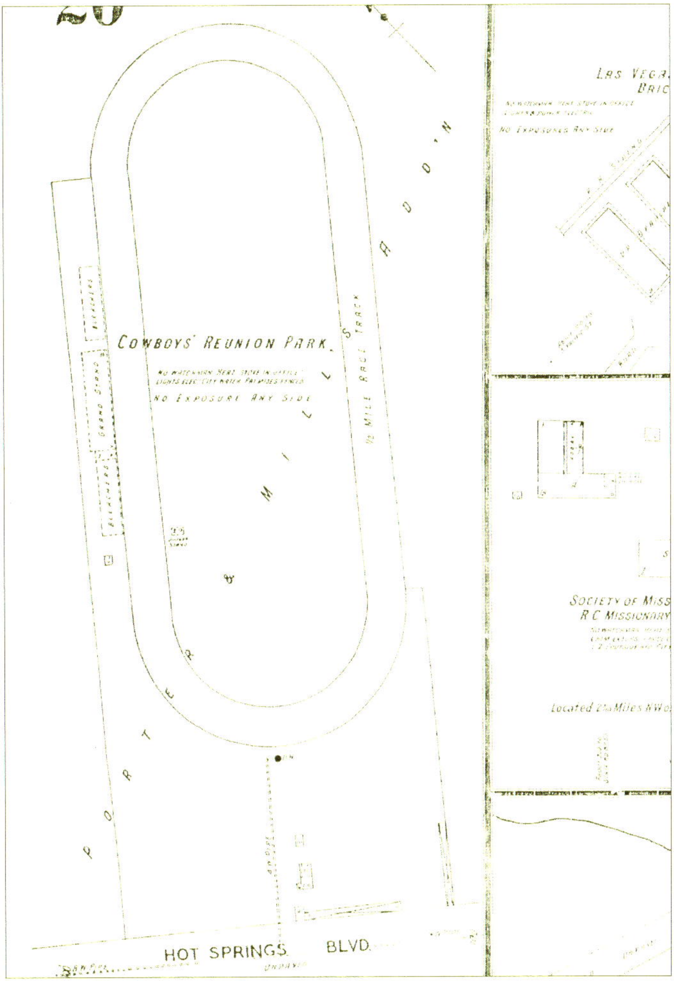

Map of Cowboys' Reunion Park on Hot Springs Boulevard: one-half-mile racetrack, arena, grandstand, bleachers, and judges' stand. *Courtesy City of Las Vegas Museum and Rough Rider Memorial Collection, 500.18.*

Cowboy Reunions of Las Vegas, New Mexico

Map showing the City of Las Vegas, the Town of Las Vegas, and Cowboys' Reunion Park, located west of the Gallinas River and north of the Old Town Plaza Park. *Courtesy City of Las Vegas Museum and Rough Rider Memorial Collection, 500.18.*

COWBOY REUNIONS OF LAS VEGAS, NEW MEXICO

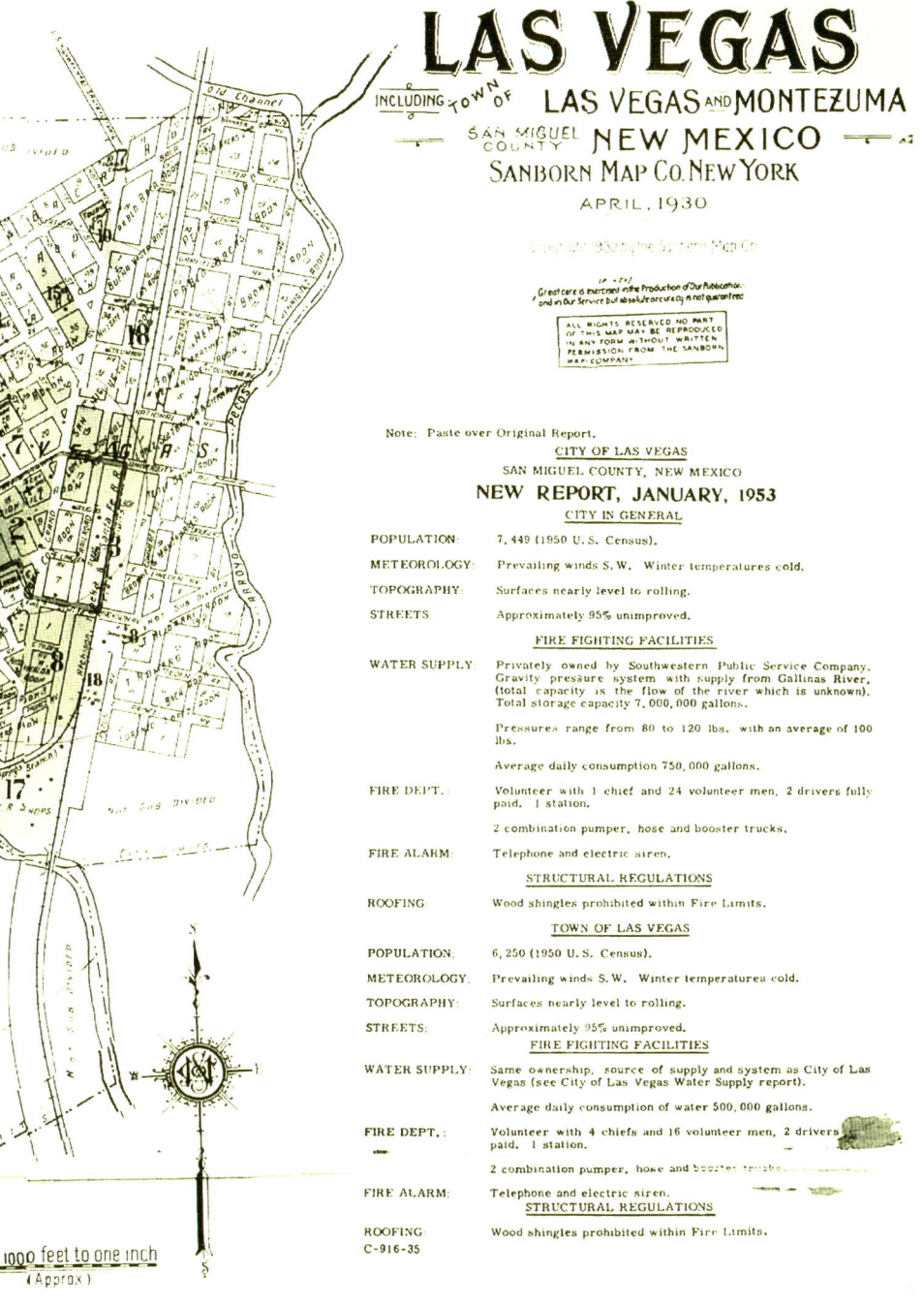

LAS VEGAS
INCLUDING TOWN OF LAS VEGAS AND MONTEZUMA
SAN MIGUEL COUNTY NEW MEXICO
SANBORN MAP CO. NEW YORK
APRIL, 1930

Note: Paste over Original Report.
CITY OF LAS VEGAS
SAN MIGUEL COUNTY, NEW MEXICO

NEW REPORT, JANUARY, 1953
CITY IN GENERAL

POPULATION:	7,449 (1950 U.S. Census).
METEOROLOGY:	Prevailing winds S.W. Winter temperatures cold.
TOPOGRAPHY:	Surfaces nearly level to rolling.
STREETS:	Approximately 95% unimproved.

FIRE FIGHTING FACILITIES

WATER SUPPLY:	Privately owned by Southwestern Public Service Company. Gravity pressure system with supply from Gallinas River, (total capacity is the flow of the river which is unknown). Total storage capacity 7,000,000 gallons.
	Pressures range from 80 to 120 lbs. with an average of 100 lbs.
	Average daily consumption 750,000 gallons.
FIRE DEPT.:	Volunteer with 1 chief and 24 volunteer men, 2 drivers fully paid. 1 station.
	2 combination pumper, hose and booster trucks.
FIRE ALARM:	Telephone and electric siren.

STRUCTURAL REGULATIONS

ROOFING	Wood shingles prohibited within Fire Limits.

TOWN OF LAS VEGAS

POPULATION:	6,250 (1950 U.S. Census).
METEOROLOGY:	Prevailing winds S.W. Winter temperatures cold.
TOPOGRAPHY:	Surfaces nearly level to rolling.
STREETS:	Approximately 95% unimproved.

FIRE FIGHTING FACILITIES

WATER SUPPLY:	Same ownership, source of supply and system as City of Las Vegas (see City of Las Vegas Water Supply report).
	Average daily consumption of water 500,000 gallons.
FIRE DEPT.:	Volunteer with 4 chiefs and 16 volunteer men, 2 drivers paid. 1 station.
	2 combination pumper, hose and booster trucks.
FIRE ALARM:	Telephone and electric siren.

STRUCTURAL REGULATIONS

ROOFING	Wood shingles prohibited within Fire Limits.

C-916-35

Reunion, the CRA updated the arena and racetrack and added a covered grandstand and new judges' booth. Before a crowd estimated at between 7,500 and 10,000, New Mexico governor William C. McDonald officially dedicated Cowboys' Park and congratulated the organizers on a job well done. According to Perrigo, the converted Gallinas Park served the reunion rodeos well until 1924, when the CRA built a new, full-service rodeo plant on Hot Springs Boulevard about one mile north of the town line at the intersection of Hot Springs and Porter Street.

As a for-profit corporation, the CRA was tightly organized, conducted timely promotions, and sought the best rodeo stock, exciting exhibition performers, and popular orchestras. The organizers were proud to proclaim and follow through with a square deal for every contestant at the rodeo. According to a report in *The Wild Bunch*, "the spirit of the square deal permeated the whole celebration" at the 1916 reunion rodeo.

Cited as an example is the story of Slim Allen, a bulldogger. Allen didn't get to compete in his first bulldogging event because he had been thrown and accidentally stomped on by his own hazing horse. The rest of the bulldoggers "got together and decided to allow Slim to have another chance on the day of finals." And he went for it. "Sore and limping, his face plastered with bandages, Slim bulldogged two steers and to the great delight of the crowd won first money by a scant few seconds."

The 1922 *Reunion News* extended the "square deal" beyond the rodeo arena by urging anyone who was overcharged for anything to report it to the "Chamber of Commerce, Reunion Headquarters, or Mayor Blood himself." But the article was quick to point out that no overcharging was expected because "our merchant folks have always been mighty fair and reasonable in this respect, but if you run into the unexpected do not hesitate to lift up your voice and Holler!—to the right officials."

No matter how square the deal or fine the facilities, it wouldn't mean a thing if people didn't know about it. So, the CRA worked hard at promotional activities. In February 1916, five months before the event, the association placed a full-page advertisement in the *Evening Herald* of Albuquerque, New Mexico, offering $5,000 in cash prizes and "contests for real hands." Illustrated by the drawings of Ruth Monro Augur, western artist and Works Progress Administration muralist, the ad focused on the roundup and invited "Cowboys! Cowgirls! and Humans!" to partake in a "Real Show and a Square Deal to All." The advertisement included a listing of rodeo events: steer roping and riding, bulldogging, relay and quick-change races, trick riding, bronc-riding cowgirls and cowboys, and chuck wagon and potato races. As added inducement, everyone was promised a rip-roaring good time and plenty of chances to "say howdy" to old friends.

The CRA also advertised and followed up with after-event reports in the *Las Vegas Daily Optic*, *The Wild Bunch*, and its own, short-lived, publication, *Reunion News*, written and edited by Phil LeNoir and S. Omar Barker. In addition to newspaper coverage, the CRA explored all publicity avenues open at the time. City of Las Vegas Museum records indicate that the CRA commissioned the Kansas City Slide Company to hand-paint glass slides for traveling magic lantern shows, the predecessor to slide shows, and gave away free mementos like matchbooks, souvenir ribbons, stickers, and programs. Another new marketing venture was panoramic photos, and a brief article in the *Optic* entitled "Expert Photographer to Get Reunion Views" noted that Almeron Newman of Denver, Colorado, along with six additional "experts," was scheduled to make "panorama pictures of six feet in length of the various doings at the Reunion." The photographs would be

Hand-painted glass slide for a magic lantern, a predecessor of the slide projector. Magic lantern shows were thriving publicity attractions in the nineteenth and early twentieth centuries. *Courtesy City of Las Vegas Museum and Rough Rider Memorial Collection, 66.6.1.*

displayed at the Las Vegas Light and Power Company, and postcards would be made as well. Newman became a regular at the reunions, making annual panoramic photographs of the parade participants and rodeo contestants. Postcards were another popular way to spread the word. With pictures of rodeo contests, original artwork and poetry, and rodeo schedules, the cards often crossed the country to places like Milwaukee, Wisconsin, advertising events at the Cowboys' Reunion.

Phil LeNoir often ran the publicity campaigns. For 1922, LeNoir and S. Omar Barker produced *Reunion News*. The front page featured a picture of Mayme and Leonard Stroud, each standing on two horses and performing a Roman race. Articles covered the Cowboys' Reunion and all its happenings—past and upcoming. It included definitions and explanations of rodeo events, descriptions of the dances, accolades for the previous year's reunion, and claims of "hundreds of cowboys, cowgirls, and cowmen, blocks of decorated floats, the white haired veterans of the G.A.R. and the pioneers of New Mexico—oh, cowboy!" The publication also included tales, both tall and otherwise, like "When Texas Annie Rode the Bull, a Complete Short Story Written Around the Cowboys Reunion" by Phil LeNoir and S. Omar Barker.

Sadly, the 1922 publicity campaign was the last one LeNoir conducted, for he died on January 12, 1923. The *Optic* reported that the directors of the CRA adopted a resolution expressing their appreciation for his support and friendship and conveying their sympathy to the family. According to S. Omar Barker, due to LeNoir's organizational and marketing skills, the 1921 Cowboys' Reunion "came alive as no other Reunion had ever done," and the 1922 promotion campaign "for [its] originality, color, and results has never been equalled."

One of the most effective means of promoting the event was word of mouth, and the cowhand contestants were expert tellers of tales, like the one about Smiling Bill Stanton's last ride at the Cowboys' Reunion, Slim Allen's "square deal," and Ed Gallegos's famous bootless steer ride. Although often embellished, most of the stories had some basis in truth. The July 5, 1916 *Optic* reported the following:

> *There were several wild steers ridden this morning, Ed Gallegos making the most sensational ride ever seen by the cowboys. The steer began to buck at the corral, and kept going clear past the grandstand. It used its horns to such good advantage, that Ed's boots were pulled off, but he kept his seat, and "scratched" the animal all over, with his bare feet. The cowboys who saw the performance declare that the ride was the greatest they have ever seen.*

This story alone would bring spectators on the chance that something as exciting or unusual could happen at any moment, but then there was the tale, in the July 3, 1919 *Optic*, of two outlaw broncs that jumped a corral fence: "One of the outlaws, United States, surprised the crowd and contestants alike by jumping the nine foot corral fence. [And] Bull Whiskey jumped out of the chute twice while being saddled." Then, on the fifth, the *Optic* reported on the comical goings-on during the wild horse race event: "After considerable hard work and a number of failures the unbroken mounts from the range were saddled and the race started. Several riders were practically around the track when the horses decided to go the other way and immediately followed out their intentions to the amusement of the crowd and the disgust of the cowboys."

Another story from this period that was told and retold is that of Bill Stanton's last bronc ride, written up by Phil LeNoir and circulated through the *Reunion News*. Artist Edward Borein attended several reunions with sketchpad in hand, and at the 1921 rodeo, he created his subject matter by challenging Bill Stanton to repeat his winning bronc ride, but with conditions. Borein "wagered the buckaroo he could not ride the same outlaw again with reins in teeth, and spurs scratching the bronk's shoulders at every jump." Stanton did it, and Borein caught it on paper. However, within days "came the almost unbelievable news, whispered from awed lips of puncher to puncher: Over night [after returning to Colorado,] Bill Stanton had joined the Round-Up from which no buckaroo ever returns. That ride, the ride with reins in teeth—and which Borein has immortalized [on paper], was Smiling Bill's last."

At the time, Borein's sketch appeared on rodeo posters, and nearly twenty years later, the sketch was reproduced again and graced the covers of the rodeo programs from 1940 to 1942.

Community support was essential to the success of such a large annual event, and the *Optic* reported on all of the activities, as well as daily rodeo scores. The local stores and banks closed early to allow employees to attend the festivities, and as requested by the CRA, many people donned western hats, plaid shirts, boots, and jeans. Las Vegans donated their time and whatever they could. "Parade King" Charles O'Malley, former East Las Vegas fire chief, participated in and helped organize the parades. "Lujan of Bridge Street contributed a wagonload of hay to the pageant." The Las Vegas Boy Scout Troop, "stationed at the information bureau on Railroad Avenue, escorted hundreds of persons to rooms in various parts of the city, day and night." The scouts met the trains, ushered visitors to wherever they

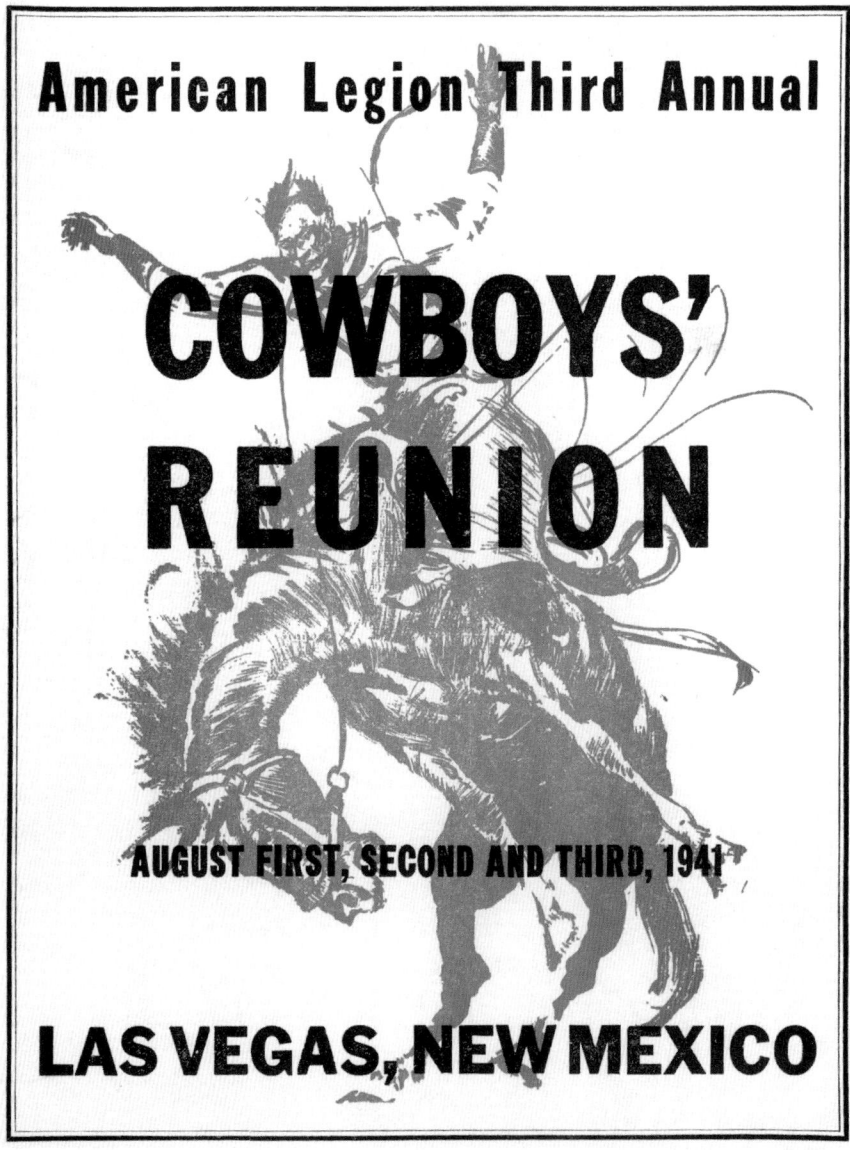

The 1940, '41, and '42 Cowboys' Reunion program covers carried reproductions of Edward Borein's original drawing of "Smiling" Bill Stanton's last ride, hands free with the reins between his teeth, in 1921. *Courtesy City of Las Vegas Museum and Rough Rider Memorial Collection 73.16.85.*

needed to go, and handed out information on hotels and restaurants. Even the utility company helped out. The Las Vegas Light and Power Company strung lights along the main streets and turned them on each night at dusk: "Las Vegas will be right there with its own white way during the time that the cowboys and their friends are in the city." By 1922, the Las Vegas and San Miguel Chamber of Commerce was lending a hand with publicity.

Until its demise in 1923, the Commercial Club continued its strong support of the reunion and rodeo through promotional activities. In 1916, the club created and distributed oblong cards with each day's rodeo schedule on one side and on the other explicit instructions for traveling by horse, wagon, or vehicle, round-trip, from Santa Rosa to Las Vegas, including important landmarks like gates, houses, trees, and available water.

Ultimately, the rodeo was a big draw all by itself. Throughout the 1910s and 1920s, the Cowboys' Reunion was the place to be, the big gathering, the "saltiest rodeo," while the reunion activities continued to attract people who wanted to reconnect with old friends and acquaintances. Everyone from the western literati and artists to working cowhands and celebrity exhibitioners managed to get themselves, their rigs, and their "togs" to the big show each year at Las Vegas on the first weekend in July. Year after year, the association made sure the rodeo had the best stock procurable in order to draw working cowhand contestants and big-name exhibition acts. But the CRA also made sure there was plenty of fun with famous clowns, donkey acts, and farcical contests such as beard-growing, pie-eating, and cakewalking.

Although most contestants rode in several events, some earned notoriety for special skills. "Powder Face" Eckerd and Fred Atkinson were considered great bulldoggers. Famous steer riders Ben Stacel and Bill Stanton visited and revisited the Cowboys' Reunion. And early bronc riders such as Bugger Red, Montana Belle, Walter Rumans, and Prairie Rose—who at that time had to saddle and mount the wild horses in the arena—came to Cowboy Park in Las Vegas.

With each new year, more cowgirls showed up, sporting flamboyant silk shirts and split skirts and riding tricked-out mounts in flowered leather tack. The cowgirls were crowd-pleasers. In addition to saddle bronc riding, trick riding, relay and chariot racing, bulldogging, and steer riding, these fearless women performed swan dives on speeding mounts and switched horses at the gallop. According to Teresa Jordan, the cowgirls' "tricks consisted of stands, drags, vaults, and anything else a rider had nerve enough to do, including going under the horse's belly at a gallop." In relay races, cowgirls changed mounts three times, some leaping from one horse to another without touching ground.

LOG--Santa Rosa to Las Vegas and Return

SANTA ROSA TO LAS VEGAS

0	Turn left around Bank corner
	Turn left past warehouse
2 M	Left hand—follow telephone line
4	Left around fence corner
6.7	Left around stone and adobe houses past little hill and thru gate
9.5	Thru iron gate
14.5	Thru iron gate
18.5	Hick's ranch. Water. Cross arroya to right
20	Turn right at post
23	Gate at corral
32.3	Thru gate and turn left
32.8	Keep to right
36.5	Thru gate straight ahead
41.5	to 43, road rough, around head of arroya and turn back left
44.3	Gate
46	To right and follow main mesa on right
54.5	Thru gate
54.8	Thru gate
55	House and trees. Water. At road sign test brakes and turn right up long hill, (the Canon del Aqua Hill)
59	Right into road
62.5	Turn left
71	LAS VEGAS

LAS VEGAS TO SANTA ROSA

0	LAS VEGAS—Turn right at Lumber Co., and cross iron bridge
.7	Keep left hand road
3.7	Right to Henrietta ranch fence corner and keep straight ahead
8.1	White house and windmill on right
8.2	Turn right into lane
13.7	Big hill—TEST BRAKES. (Canon del Aqua Hill)
15.6	Turn left at sign board—foot of hill
16	Houses and trees to right. Water
16.5	Gate
17	Gate
24	Take left
25.2	Take left
27.3	Gate
39	Right, thru iron gate
48.1	Spring. Water in tank
48.2	Corral and iron gate
50.4	Turn left to post
53.9	Hick's ranch
54.9	Turn right
58	Gate
60.5	Gate, and either road
65.5	Thru gate and turn right
68	Right, around fence corner, down fence and angle to left to
71	Warehouse. Pass, and under R. R. and left into SANTA ROSA

COMPLIMENTS
COMMERCIAL CLUB
LAS VEGAS, NEW MEXICO

Cowboy Reunions of Las Vegas, New Mexico

Not afraid to have a joke at their own expense, cowboys on horseback race a clown on a cow. *Courtesy City of Las Vegas Museum and Rough Rider Memorial Collection, 2000.16.7. Photographer: Almeron Newman.*

Previous page: In 1916, paved highways were rare in northeastern New Mexico. These directions for a round trip between Santa Rosa and Las Vegas tell a tale of the trip before and after visiting or competing at the Cowboys' Reunion. On the backside of the card was pasted the daily rodeo event schedule. It was made and distributed by the Las Vegas Commercial Club. *Courtesy City of Las Vegas Museum and Rough Rider Memorial Collection 73.16.183a.*

Although in 1916, Ladies' Bronco Riding at the Cowboys' Reunion was reported in *The Wild Bunch* as a "special exhibition," by 1917 it was listed in the rodeo schedule as an official event for both July 3 and 4. Prairie Rose Henderson, rancher and working cowgirl, who had taken the bronc-riding title at the New York Stampede of 1916, joined Prairie Lillie Allen, Texas Annie, Montana Belle, and Clyde Lindsey for the Las Vegas reunion festivities and rodeo contests. That year, Montana Belle "wowed" the crowd when "she rode an unknown bronc that made a reputation for high bucking and…she rode him with a swing to her that would do credit to the best cowboy bronc rider."

Rodeo schedules and programs indicate that throughout the first phase of the Cowboys' Reunion, there were many popular exhibition acts in addition to the contested events: trick riders Mayme and Leonard Stroud; Chief, the horse that jumps an automobile full of "livin' humans"; trick ropers Johnny Judd, Jack Ray, and Sammy Garrett; and marksman Texas George Briggs. In the early years, Frederick Mellon "Foghorn" Clancy (1882–1957) was one of

"The crowds loved the cowgirls' wild daring, their verve, their romantic beauty." Montana Belle trick riding at the second Cowboys' Reunion Rodeo. She also competed in bronc riding. *Courtesy Citizens' Committee for Historic Preservation, Annabelle Lucero Collection.*

the official announcers for rodeo events. Former United States scout Colonel W.B. "Idaho Bill" Pearson (1868–1942) provided stock, and until the late 1920s, rodeo producer, rancher, stockman, and charter member of the Cowboys' Reunion Association "Tex" Austin (1886–1938) directed the whole affair. An additional attraction was the steady increase in prize monies from $5,000 in 1915 and 1916 to $15,000 by 1928 and the added "Championship Trophies."

Artists, songwriters, poets, and writers glorified the reunion and helped spread the word. One major contributor to the event's glamour and appeal was N. Howard "Jack" Thorp (1867–1940), one of the first collectors and publishers of cowboy lyrics and poetry, as found in his 1908 book *Songs of the Cowboys*. His second edition, in 1921, included several song lyrics that he picked up at the Cowboys' Reunion in Las Vegas, as well as his original composition, "Las Vegas Reunion," a song detailing the event. His call to "Cow-girls from far Montana/En the little Prairie Rose," his references to the Meadow City, and his bow to the changing rural culture—"But [auto]'mobiles come by thousands"—fix the reunion in time and enhance the mystique of the American West. During his visit, Thorp collected songs from Phil LeNoir and anonymous donors—one identified simply as "a young lady at the Cowboys' Reunion at Las Vegas, New Mexico."

The artwork and photography of many visiting American artists also contributed to the continued success. Many of the artists who displayed their works or created pieces especially for the reunion became famous for popularizing the West and the real work of the ranch hand. Will James (1892–1942), illustrator and author, began sketching at age four and was best known for his Newberry Medal–winning book *Smoky the Cow Horse*. In collaboration with Phil LeNoir, James's illustrative drawing enhanced a postcard for the 1924 rodeo. The works of Ruth Monro Augur (1886–1967) and Randall Davey (1887–1964) illustrated and spread the appeal of all things western, especially the Las Vegas Cowboys' Reunion events. Davey and Augur studied with Robert Henri in New York but were drawn to the Southwest for subjects. Davey produced an original etching, *Wild Horses—Cow Boys Reunion*, for the rodeo, and Augur's drawings were used to illustrate the 1916 *Evening Herald* advertisement. According to the official program of 1928, the paintings of Gerald Cassidy (1879–1934), who had already achieved international recognition, were featured at the Las Vegas First National Bank Building art exhibit in conjunction with the Cowboys' Reunion. Edward Borein (1872–1945), a rancher himself, began drawing at age five and became famous for accurate, rather than romanticized, depictions of the vanishing western America. Several of Borein's drawings were used for programs and poster.

Wild Horses—Cow Boys Reunion. Etching by Randall Davey, circa 1920–21. The reunions at Las Vegas attracted soon-to-be famous artists from throughout the country. *Courtesy City of Las Vegas Museum and Rough Rider Memorial Collection, 2010.6.1.*

Cowboy Reunions of Las Vegas, New Mexico

DRAWING BY WILL JAMES

DOWN ON THE OL' BAR-G
By Phil LeNoir

The boss he took a trip to France,
   Down on the ol' Bar-G.
An' left his gal to run the ranch,
   Down on the ol' Bar-G.
She wouldn't let us chew nor cuss,
Had to keep slicked up like a city bus,
So round-up time was u-nan-i-muss—
   Down on the ol' Bar-G.

Our round-up cook, he soon got th'u,
   Down on the ol' Bar-G.
Fou d his clay pipe right in the stew,
   Down on the ol' Bar-G.
But when we let that feller go
We married grief an' we married woe,
For the gal opined *she'd* bake the dough,
   Down on the ol' Bar-G.

Wisht you'd seen her openin' meal
   Down on the ol' Bar-G.
We all blinked twict—seemed plumb unreal,
   Down on the ol' Bar-G.
Thar was figs an' fudge and whipped-up pru-in
An' angel cake all dipped in goo-in,
"My Gawd" said Tex, "My stomick's ruint"—
   Down on the ol' Bar-G.

We quit that job an' cook-ladee,
   Down on the ol' Bar-G.
An' pulled our freight for the lone prairee,
   Down on the ol' Bar-G.
For out on the range we could chew and cuss,
An' git real mean and bois-ter-uss,
Whar apron-strings they couldn't rope us.
   Down on the ol' Bar-G.

—POETRY: A MAGAZINE OF VERSE

COPYRIGHTED 1922 PHIL H. LENOIR

Promotional postcard, with reproduction of a Will James drawing and "Down on the Ol' Bar G" by Phil LeNoir, Commercial Club secretary, Cowboys' Reunion rodeo general chairman, and creator of the first slogan, "Git fer Vegas, Cowboy!" *Courtesy City of Las Vegas Museum and Rough Rider Memorial Collection, 73.16.77.*

There were always stories to be told and lyrics to be written or sung. The *Optic* of July 11, 1916, published an eight-stanza lyrical poem entitled "Hermit Lee" by Pascal Bozeman. This piece relates the legend of the hermit and the local mountain peak named for him. It contains these lines:

Where the air is pure and light;
Where the mountains shine like an old slick dime,
And the clouds are out of sight—

Local authors drew inspiration from the annual doings as well. Phil LeNoir (1882–1923) produced poetry, song lyrics, fiction, and nonfiction. Some of his titles include *Rhymes of the Wild and Woolly*, "Down on the Ol' Bar G," and "The Finger of Billy the Kid." Dee Bibb (1893–1968), local musician, champion bulldogger, and raconteur, participated in both phases of the reunion—as a contestant in the 1920s and again as a contestant-organizer from the 1940s to the 1960s. S. Omar Barker (1894–1985), soldier, rancher, poet, prolific regional writer, and longtime promoter of all phases of the Cowboys' Reunion, wrote about the events and served as publicity agent in the 1920s. Barker continued to cover the Cowboys' Reunion for *New Mexico Magazine* in the 1940s and '50s.

The dances and musical entertainment were big draws for the re-unionizers. The 1928 rodeo program announced the doings of various bands in attendance that year. The 120th Engineers Band, the Cowboys' Band, and Kasper's Band were contracted to play daily at designated places throughout the east and west sides of the river and at Cowboys' Park. In 1925, the Cowboys' Band had grown to thirty-two pieces. Once touted in the *Optic* as "the most famous organization of its kind in the West," in addition to its reunion gigs, the band traveled its own circuit. Both Callon and Perrigo report that in 1924 rodeo director "Tex" Austin began a huge national and international promotion, part of which included taking the band on an extended tour of the United States and London, England. Although no figures are available, the *Optic* noted that the 1925 Cowboys' Reunion rodeo, following the band's big tour, was "the largest ever."

At the balls, the elected queen of the reunion started things off with a grand march. In 1917, the *Optic* reported that the first night's dance, opened by Audrey Burns, enjoyed "the best social time of the reunion":

A tremendous crowd attended the cowboys' dance last night at the Duncan opera house. When the grand march began the space reserved for spectators

> *was filled, upstairs and down, and the dancing floor was jammed. The Simison orchestra, which was in fine form, furnished the music, which was such as to inspire everybody to dance.*
>
> *The cowboys didn't care a hang for expenses, and they let the dancers have all of the encores they wanted. It was not until 2 o'clock this morning that the last dance was played. And a big crowd was on the floor when the affair closed.*

That year, the reunion held dances at both the opera house and the armory, and by 1922, two dances each night were held. According to *Reunion News*, "[B]oth halls will have cracking fine orchestras."

By most accounts, the Cowboys' Reunion at Las Vegas thrived throughout the 1920s. It seemed unstoppable. World War I, recessions, prohibition, and the growing mechanization of ranch work did not deter its momentum. Some modern conveniences were absorbed, like Johnny Judd's exhibition act, "bulldogging from an auto," and horses willing and able to jump over cars. Each Cowboys' Reunion and rodeo were billed as bigger, better, and saltier than the previous one until, in the words of S. Omar Barker, the "old Reunion...stepped in a patch of gopher holes called Depression, busted both front legs and had to be shot."

The official daily program of July 5, 1931, which may represent the final rodeo of the first phase, proclaimed it to be the Seventeenth Annual Cowboys' Reunion and listed officers, board members, and judges. Ten events in addition to the "Grand Entry," a "Clown and Trick Mule" exhibition, and a "Business Men's Special" race were scheduled that day, and there were "special evening events" to be announced. The official reunion dance took place at the armory with the music of the "Melodylanders Official Reunion Orchestra." A photograph published in the *Our Lady of Sorrows Weekly Bulletin* shows a large crowd in the grandstand, with Governor Dillon and Judge Armijo in attendance.

Sources vary about when and why the rodeo gates closed on this first phase of the Cowboys' Reunion. Barker put it at 1930. In the *Optic*'s sixtieth-anniversary insert of June 3, 1939, Jack Knight reported that "local interest waned, and in 1932, it was decided to discontinue. The grounds were dismantled, and to all purposes the Cowboy's Reunion passed into history." Milton Callon and the Cowboys' Reunion program of 1948 identified the end of the first phase as 1930; Perrigo stated that in spite of adding stock car racing and polo, "attendance declined. After 1933, the rodeos were suspended." The existence of the Seventeenth Annual Cowboys' Reunion rodeo program makes a sure-fire statement that the reunion and rodeo events took place that year.

As for the reasons the reunions ceased, some blamed the Depression, while others cited a lack of public interest. National events of the times took their toll. The Wall Street stock market crashed on October 29, 1929, but drought, culminating in the American Dust Bowl, and repeated recessions and unemployment lasted until the United States entered World War II. This combination of disasters devastated small towns across America and made people less enthusiastic or financially able to support and participate in large-scale events like the Cowboys' Reunion.

Whatever the causes of its end, during its heyday, the first phase of the Cowboys' Reunion at Las Vegas earned a reputation as the "Saltiest Rodeo on Earth." It brought together rural families and townspeople and provided music, art, literature, fine food, and rodeo along with excellent stock, cowhand contestants, flashy cowgirls, and celebrity exhibitions. The organizers promoted the event almost year round. Major media attention came from *The Wild Bunch* periodical, "Devoted to Ranches, Roundups, Stampedes and Wild West Exclusively," as well as additional popular

Salute to the audience. *From right to left*: Walt Naylor, first Cowboys' Reunion Association president; Colonel "Idaho Bill" Pearson, stock producer; and Tex Austin, rodeo promoter. Postcard, 1916. *Courtesy City of Las Vegas Museum and Rough Rider Memorial Collection, 64.63.3. Photographer: Almeron Newman.*

marketing of the day, like traveling magic lantern shows, promotional tours, panoramic photographs, artists' renditions, poetry, postcards, short stories, and the old standard—word of mouth. Throughout its first phase, the Cowboys' Reunion rodeo offered a square deal for all, rollicking good times, and a real "get-togetherness." In the words of Phil LeNoir:

> *Contrary to the general impression, the Cowboys Reunion is not a Wild West Circus. The majority of the performers are real-for-sure cowboys who once a year don their work-a-day outfits—their chaps, spurs and sombreros—and "burn the wind" for Las Vegas in the Reunion ranch and round-up games against all comers.*
>
> *The Las Vegas Celebration can be said to be even more than a Contest. It is a Re-union: a Re-union of the old timers who once again "hark back" to the [18]60s, the 70s, the 80s. Ranch families separated for a year, perhaps many years, may be seen camped along the trouted snow-fed streams of Gallinas Canyon.*

Indeed, as one of the 1922 promotional flyers proclaimed, the Las Vegas Cowboys' Reunion was "More than a Rodeo." It was a way for folks to neighbor again.

"Let's Revive the Reunion," 1939–1951

This year, Leonard Hoskins Post 24, American Legion, will revive the reunion in a three-day event guaranteed to be packed with thrills.
—Las Vegas Daily Optic

The year 1939 started out on a hopeful note. The country's economy was on the mend, employment was on the rise, and, inconceivable in retrospect, it seemed that the United States might avoid entering another world war. Las Vegans nurtured a similar optimism and worked toward making a brighter future by improving their economic base. Bringing back the Cowboys' Reunion, in response to Walter Vivian's repeated pleas of "Let's Revive the Reunion," became part of that brighter future. But 1939 also marked a turning point for what was quickly becoming the professional sport of rodeo, and this would have unforeseen effects on the Cowboys' Reunion as a whole but especially on the rodeo.

The American Legion's Leonard Hoskins Post No. 24, named for the first soldier from San Miguel County to die in World War I, answered Vivian's call. According to Jack Knight's article "Expect Rodeo to Bring Many Visitors Here" in the *Optic*, the Legionnaires reestablished the reunion in a desire to "bring back the vast hordes of visitors" that the first phase of the Cowboys' Reunion had generated and thus revitalize tourist potential. The Legionnaires saw it as a "civic undertaking." But it was not an easy task. Although no specifics were mentioned, the 1941 rodeo program notes, "The Legion's efforts were somewhat scorned at the beginning, although the

Cowboys' Reunion parade, 1939, the first reunion sponsored by Leonard Hoskins Post 24 of the American Legion, Douglas Avenue. *Courtesy City of Las Vegas Museum and Rough Rider Memorial Collection, 73.16.112. Photo credit: Rex Studio.*

majority of the citizens cooperated and harbored a hope that the Legion would succeed."

From early on, the Legion's work in reviving the reunion illustrated a tension regarding the nature and mission of the renewed Cowboys' Reunion. The 1940 rodeo program notes, "The American Legion intends to build this Cowboys' Reunion into one of the largest and best in the whole Southwest and to keep it strictly for the ranch hands of the Southwest." At this point, the Legion recognized that the reunion rodeo was "not a great profit-making project" but rather an event "given by Cowboys, for Cowboys." However, the Legion was trying to reestablish the reunion based on the mission and vision of 1915 in the rodeo world of the 1940s, and as Fredriksson points out, rodeo events and expectations were moving rapidly in a direction that would define "the largest and the best" based on criteria established through professional, financial, and athletic standards. Ultimately, the Legion would focus more on the rodeo than the "re-unionizing."

In 1939, however, the revived Cowboys' Reunion and its organizers enthusiastically approached bringing back "get-togetherness," good times, dances, parades, and "one of the largest and best" working cowboy rodeos in the Southwest. In addition to the Legion's stated purposes, the revived reunion strengthened the sometimes tenuous connection between the two Las Vegas communities. Both mayors warmly welcomed the event, and in the 1940 rodeo program, M.A. Romero, mayor of the Town of Las Vegas, noted, "The people of the Town of Las Vegas…are part of the homefolks who have always been happy to invite the world to join in the annual Cowboys' Reunion." The *Optic* and official rodeo programs began referring to the two communities as Greater Las Vegas.

Added to the Legion's efforts were various changes happening within the larger rodeo community. In 1936, the Cowboys' Turtle Association (CTA), named for the popular use of turtleneck jerseys among cowboys, was established, and according to Fredriksson, it helped develop rodeo rules and regulations: "By 1939, the rodeo cowboy had…prescribed and enforced rules that he himself had been instrumental in formulating. His future looked promising."

Throughout the '30s and into the '40s, cowboys and cowgirls struggled to establish fair treatment in the growing world of spectator-sport rodeo. Furthermore, as rodeo became recognized for its athleticism and as a source of income, competition became keener and the rodeo cowboys and cowgirls began taking themselves and their efforts more seriously. For earlier contestants, rodeo had been "the play" of the working cowhand. These major nationwide shifts trickled down to the regional rodeos as spectators demanded bigger and more exciting shows.

Las Vegas was no exception. The American Legion's revival of the Cowboys' Reunion struggled to define its identity within the shifting dust of the larger rodeo world. The rodeo maintained its status as a working cowhand-ranch rodeo but tried to keep up with the demands of the growing professional and nationally popular sport. To this end, the Legion enlisted the help of professional rodeo production companies, added new events, led major publicity campaigns, and built a new rodeo arena. All of these efforts filled the new grandstand.

Although the basic structure of the three-day Cowboys' Reunion event remained the same, the Legionnaires made some significant changes. In the hopes of ensuring success in 1939, the Legion established a task force headed by Frank Vaughn and J.O. Atkinson, built a new rodeo arena, offered $3,000 with entry fees added as prize money, and hired well-known rodeo producer Johnny Mullins of El Paso to direct the arena activities and bring in the bucking horses. Mullins had already made a name for himself producing rodeos and providing stock throughout the Southwest. The *Optic* reported that for the 1939 rodeo, Mullins "promised to bring his top string of horses to Las Vegas and claims they are the saltiest he has ever assembled." Mullins also announced that he'd have Brahma bulls for riding, Mexican steers for bulldogging, and "plenty of fast calves."

Unlike the Cowboys' Reunion Association of 1915, the Legionnaires did not create a separate, for-profit corporation but rather sought underwriters from among the business community. In this way, they avoided asking for donations from the local businesses, still reeling from years of depression and drought. To raise funds and call attention to the big event, Legionnaires made countless booster trips throughout New Mexico and the Southwest and advertised regionally.

To begin with, the Legion hired Joe Atkinson and Ed Connery, who had worked on the Madison Square Garden Rodeo, to design the new modern facility. In *New Mexico Magazine*, Charles Dingus reported that "Legionnaires long unused to hard work got out and sawed and hammered, and built the rodeo grounds." The new arena boasted a racetrack, several animal chutes, and a grandstand that could accommodate four thousand. A major innovation at the rodeo grounds was in the stock loading area. The addition of bucking chutes and loading corrals promised to shorten the time between contests and speed up the entire show, providing a "fast, snappy rodeo, presented with showmanship and color." With updating and maintenance, the Legion Park Rodeo Grounds would draw and accommodate large crowds until the late 1960s. Located at the corner of Seventh Street and Legion Drive, the rodeo grounds helped spread and develop the two communities northward.

For the revival, the new sponsors changed not only the rodeo location but also the meeting dates, the title of the event, and the annual numbering system. The bright blue program cover of 1939 proudly proclaimed "American Legion First Annual Cowboys' Reunion, August 4, 5, and 6." Thereafter, until the mid-1960s, each reunion was held during the first weekend in August, and by 1967, the count would be up to twenty-nine annual reunions. Although the prize money offered for the Legion's debut rodeo was smaller than that of the 1915 CRA rodeo, Jack Knight was optimistic: "This is large enough to attract the cream of the cowboy contest hands and with the many novelty acts that have been contracted, the Reunion is sure to be an outstanding success."

With each new year, the American Legion Cowboys' Reunion expanded. The 1945 *Optic* rodeo edition proclaimed that the Legion had faced and overcome several obstacles but that the revived Cowboys' Reunion rodeo "surpassed even the fondest expectations of the most optimistic." Each year, the rodeo was "bigger and better," and the Legion expanded its rodeo activities by "adding more equipment to the rodeo grounds, getting more publicity, gaining more momentum, and gaining the support of the entire New Mexico populace."

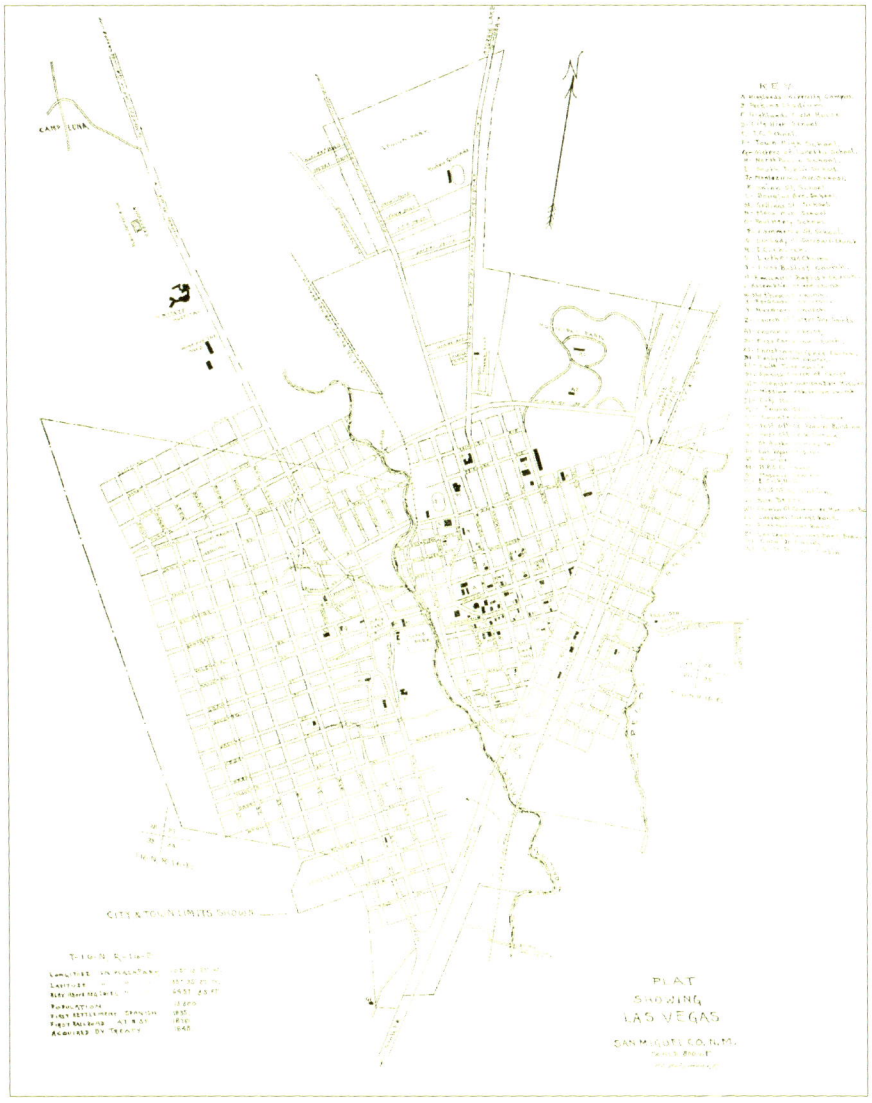

Plat map of the city and the town of Las Vegas, 1950, showing rodeo grounds at Legion Park built by the Legionnaires and volunteers for the 1939 Cowboys' Reunion revival. Prepared by H.E. Beisman, C.E., for Las Vegas–San Miguel Chamber of Commerce. *Courtesy City of Las Vegas Museum and Rough Rider Memorial Collection.*

Reunion advertising promised that the revival of "New Mexico's Most Famous Frontier Show" would have fireworks, "Every known rodeo event," champion-level contestants, "Dancing every night in western setting," "Top hands in a thrilling revival of the West's most famous Rodeo," and "Plenty of accommodations for visitors in Las Vegas, in the heart of the picturesque cow country."

Programs and posters for the revived rodeo were more colorful and flashier than those of the first phase. They often included fancy graphics, reproductions of cattle brands, and original photography. Giveaway items included souvenir ribbons and matchbooks. At the rodeo sessions, efficient and squared-away reunion staff members were easily spotted everywhere in their bright-green shirts with pearl buttons and yellow embroidered lettering.

Another major form of promotion for the rodeo came from the *Optic*. The local newspaper was a great booster of the big event. In his daily column, Editor Vivian had campaigned for close to a year to bring back the Cowboys' Reunion, and throughout the 1940s and '50s, the *Optic* provided special Cowboys' Reunion editions. These six-page inserts presented action photographs of famous rodeo contestants and exhibition acts, local advertisements professing enthusiastic support of all reunion events, informal historical articles, cowboy poetry, and profiles of participants and supporters. The August 2, 1945 *Optic* proclaimed, "Dee Bibb, who has been called the 'All-American Cowboy' will be among the old-time cowboys assisting in the arena…Dee, the tall lanky fellow with bow legs and a grin a mile wide has traveled far and wide to attend rodeos, playing a guitar and singing songs."

Bibb, transplanted to New Mexico from Oklahoma, was one of the cowboys who contested in both phases of the Cowboys' Reunion. He continued his support during the revival by helping wherever needed, always ready with his guitar. In the 1940s and '50s, there were many attendees who had seen Bibb compete in the early years and looked forward to his singing and storytelling: "Former Reunion visitors will remember Dee flying after a steer, leaping from his horse and 'rassling' the long-horned tough-necked beast to its side in a matter of seconds—because Dee was a champion and a crowd-pleaser, always willing to try to break a record and give the crowd a thrill." According to the article, Bibb "could still fork [mount] a horse and rides as though he were part of the saddle, but his chief delight is strumming the guitar and spinning yarns."

As in the Cowboys' Reunion Association phase, everything started off with a big, impressive parade. Once again, cowboys, cowgirls, horses, floats, and marching bands promenaded down the main streets of Las Vegas. And again, the two towns entered into the Wild West spirit. Businesses closed early so that employees could take part, and the townspeople put on their best western togs. Charles Dingus wrote, "Reunion days have been bringing the cowhands to Las Vegas since 1915. To start the celebration…is a parade, and the whole town turns out."

Although the parades started things off and the roundup was always a major feature, the Cowboys' Reunion was still "More than a Rodeo." It was a reunion, bringing together ranchers, cowhands, families, and city folk to get reacquainted or strengthen old ties—in other words, "to neighbor." The American Legion Cowboys' Reunion, with the community pitching in, provided all the traditional reunion events like dinners, dances, fireworks, barbecues, and opportunities for spontaneous gatherings with lots of time for "neighboring." From the *Optic*:

> *After the show, then what?*
> *That may be a question you ask concerning the rodeo performers.*
> *Well, you'll find them gathered around the corral, a hotel lobby or some other public place. If at the corral, they'll be squatted on their cowboy heels, or if at the hotel lobby, lounging in chairs, or perhaps leaning over a bar. And the conversations will be entirely rodeo. They'll discuss times, the meanest broncs, the best roping exhibition, or why some rider got hurt.*

The first phase had attracted musicians, artists, and writers, and the revival was no different. These vital, non-rodeo people made significant contributions to the fun and excitement. Newspapers, rodeo programs, and magazines reprinted generic cowboy poetry as part of the reunion promotions. Additionally, new images and poetry, often humorous, were created on the spot. S. Omar Barker, one of the reunioners who experienced both phases, supplied many reprints of his special brand of cowboy poetry, but in the 1948 rodeo program, Barker offered an original poem written for local cowboy Dee Bibb:

> *"Accordin' to Dee"*
>
> *I asked Dee Bibb to give me just a sober line or two*
> *About the workin' habits of the western buckaroo.*
> *He sorter hunched his shoulders an' he sorter ducked his head,*
> *Then give me that ol' grin of his, an' this is what he said:*
> *"The way us punchers handle bears, in case there's one about,*
> *Is grab the booger by the tongue an' yank him wrong side out.*
> *Us wild, unworried waddies, any day we're feelin' right,*
> *Can lick a wolf barehanded, an' give the wolf first bite!*

> *Our recipe for rattlesnakes—a quick an' painless death—*
> *Is drink some Injun whisky, an' then let 'em smell our breath.*
> *Them there's the kind of woolly yarns us punchers love to tell,*
> *ARn'* [sic] *is you dare to doubt 'em we'll git mad as sure as hell!*
> *But when it comes to bustin' broncs, let's lay all jokes aside:*
> *There ain't no other way, I claim, except git on an' ride!"*

Additional contributing writers and poets during this period included Walter Vivian and Charles Dingus. Both men were nonfiction writers and added to the stock of literature written about the Cowboys' Reunion events and the rodeo.

Major artists associated with the revival period included M.J. Davis, famous for his illustrated book *Sore in the Saddle*; Edward Borein, another veteran of the CRA days who captured eight-second rides in his sketchpads; and Robert K. Abbett, whose excellent painting of a saddle bronc ride graced the rodeo program covers of 1963 and 1964. The 1950 rodeo souvenir program included Davis's full-page drawing of the Las Vegas Cowboys' Reunion. Borein's drawing of Bill Stanton's last ride, originally made in 1921, was featured on the rodeo program covers from 1940 to 1942.

Photographers swarmed to all the activities, but they seemed to have concentrated on the rodeo, providing action photos of contestants, as well as publicity shots for newspapers and souvenir programs. With cameras and wooden stands, they were always on hand to catch that one-of-a-kind image of a crow-hopping bronc, a runaway bull, or square-dancing on horseback. Gone were the days of the huge panoramas of contestants lined up on horseback, but local photographers H.L. Jones, as well as the Hainlen Studio and the Rex Studio, captured snapshots of wild rides, grandstand crowds, and the ever-popular parade.

During the revival period, numerous dances were held in various locations, including the Rialto Ballroom on Bridge Street and the Meadows Hotel (currently El Fidel Hotel) Ball Room. There were also "Free Street Dances on Douglas [Avenue] Between Grand and Sixth." Individual organizations helped out the cause by sponsoring the dances and dinners. The July 31, 1947 *Optic* reported that two bands, Ned and His Melody Busters and Los Nativos of Santa Fe, would be playing at Joe's Ringside Inn on South Grand Avenue. In 1951, Al Thrasher and His Orchestra performed at the Castañeda Hotel's American Legion Ballroom, sponsored by the Las Vegas Lions Club. But the rodeo association still maintained its own Dance Committee, and in the 1948 program, its chairman, H.C. Thompson, enthusiastically invited everyone to "[k]ick your troubles in the old ashcan and fill yourself with fun" at four dances featuring two famous bands: the "'Heastonaires, stars of radio stage and screen, and 'The 7 Notes' who dish it out tailor-made to your taste." The dances that year were held at the armory and at the Officers' Club at Camp Luna.

One of the effects of the changes taking place in the larger rodeo world that had a bearing on the Cowboys' Reunion was the plight of the cowgirls. In the early CRA years, the cowgirls had always been a big draw with their flashy outfits, their daring rides, and their spunk. According to Teresa Jordan in *Cowgirls*, in the late 1930s and by the close of World War II, rodeo promoters and producers had begun dropping ladies' bronc riding and cutting other women's events from their shows due to an overabundance of chivalry, citing the dangers. However, it was and is a dangerous sport for both genders. Other reasons given for the diminishing opportunities for cowgirl contestants included the American focus on employing the returning soldiers.

Even though the Cowboys' Turtle Association (CTA) included cowgirls in its ranks and mission, the later organizations did not. Ultimately, the cowboys and cowgirls split, forming separate organizations. According to Richard Slatta in *The Cowboy Encyclopedia*, during the early 1940s, cowboy singing star Gene Autry, who had taken control of the major rodeos, eliminated women's bronc riding from competitions in New York and Boston. Soon, the other big shows followed his lead, changing the nature of cowgirl contests and eliminating competitions between cowgirls and cowboys. The American Legion Cowboys' Reunion rodeos drew cowgirl exhibition performers Clyde Lindsey and Mayme Stroud and Virginia Reger to its events for cowgirls such as girls' races, trick and exhibition riding, and the rodeo queen competitions and activities, which involved both personality and horsemanship. In later years, as the cowgirls organized and barrel racing became a sanctioned rodeo event, it also entered the Cowboys' Reunion rodeo schedule.

Rodeo in general was taking another major turn on its road to professional sport. According to Fredriksson, sometime in the mid-1940s, the rodeo cowboy came into his own, and "more cowboys than ever were making their living by competing in rodeos, not just entering for a lark." Additionally, during the late 1940s and early 1950s, rodeo as a spectator sport was receiving countrywide attention. In fact, Fredriksson refers to the '50s as "the golden age of rodeo." In turn, this national attention drew many nonworking cowboys—that is, cowboys who trained as athletes to compete in rodeo events but did not work on ranches. Las Vegas and the American Legion were following a national trend by bringing back the Cowboys' Reunion rodeo.

Cowgirls, who worked the range and competed in rodeos, were known for their fancy boots and flashy outfits, including a variety of hat styles and sizes. Nin and Louella Sims, Moon Ranch, circa 1922. *Courtesy City of Las Vegas Museum and Rough Rider Memorial Collection 2010.1.131.*

The Cowboys' Reunion rodeo program of 1948 noted, "Each succeeding year more expenditures have been necessary with larger purses to attract the cream of the rodeo circuit," indicating that the Cowboys' Reunion rodeo was no longer "the play of the working cowboy" but rather was focused on pleasing the crowds and generating profits. For the audiences, things were just as exciting, if not more so, as the Cowboys' Reunion rodeo attracted contestants from throughout the country: "There were so many contestants last year [1940] that some of the events had to be conducted before and after the regular show...Cowboys of half a dozen states wound up in the money: New Mexico, Texas, Arizona, Florida, Colorado and Nebraska."

The 1940 daily schedule of events for the rodeo listed 133 contestants—33 from outside New Mexico and 30 from Las Vegas. In 1946, 10 out of 76 contestants were Las Vegans, but by 1960, after years of big rodeo producers, 10 out of 93 contestants were from Greater Las Vegas. Rodeo events of 1940 included, in addition to novelty and exhibition acts, bronc riding, bareback bronc riding, calf roping, a variety of races, bulldogging, and Brahma bull riding. The headliners that year were Lloyd and Blanche McBee performing fancy roping and riding.

The 1940s saw traditional rodeo events merge with the newer and bigger attractions. One of the highly skilled rodeo events of 1940 was the square dance on horseback, directed by Las Vegan Ray Dukeminier. There was a children's set and an adult set, each with ten contestants on horseback, or five couples. Through the help of the local store Hoffman & Graubarth, Levi Strauss outfitted the girls and Lee Company outfitted the boys. In 1946, the climax of the first day's rodeo program, performed before "record crowds," was the daring and often dangerous quick-change race—"won by Ernesto Tapia and Shelley Hays."

The revived Cowboys' Reunion packed the new grandstand. Bull riding at Rodeo Grounds, Legion Park, North Seventh Street and Legion Drive. *Courtesy City of Las Vegas Museum and Rough Rider Memorial Collection, 73.16.123.*

Revival audiences overflowed into the bleachers. Bulldogging, Rodeo Grounds, Legion Park, North Seventh Street and Legion Drive. *Courtesy City of Las Vegas Museum and Rough Rider Memorial Collection, 73.16.125.*

Bronc riding, 1939, Rodeo Grounds, Legion Park, North Seventh Street and Legion Drive. *Courtesy City of Las Vegas Museum and Rough Rider Memorial Collection, 73.16.119. Photo credit: Morgan Photo. Photographer: Paul Odor.*

By 1945, the *Optic* was reporting that the dedicated work of Post No. 24's membership had restored the Cowboys' Reunion rodeo to "one of the outstanding rodeos in the West":

> *In each succeeding year, the Legion has presented a bigger and better three-day performance, expanding activities, adding more equipment to the rodeo grounds, getting more publicity, gaining more momentum, and gaining more support* [from] *the entire New Mexico populace.*

Out of the chutes, circa 1930s, Rodeo Grounds, Legion Park, North Seventh Street and Legion Drive. *Courtesy City of Las Vegas Museum and Rough Rider Memorial Collection, 73.16.122.*

Champion Ernesto Tapia of Las Vegas, tying a calf at the Cowboys' Reunion rodeo, circa 1950s, Legion Park Arena. *Courtesy Elsie Tapia Private Collection.*

Something new at the Cowboys' Reunion Rodeo: square dancing on horseback, circa 1930s. *Courtesy City of Las Vegas Museum and Rough Rider Memorial Collection, 73.16.134.* Photo credit: Hainlen Photo.

In the rodeo program for 1945, Lynn Beutler's name appears as the arena director, and in subsequent years until 1952, the three Beutler brothers produced the Cowboys' Reunion rodeos. Elra, Jake, and Lynn Beutler of Elk City, Oklahoma, had earned a reputation for "fast moving, hard hitting performances." Dianna Everett's profile of the organization indicates that, begun in 1929, the Beutler Brothers Company ultimately became known as "the world's largest producer of rodeos." Two major features of Beutler Brothers Company rodeos were excellent stock ("a cowboy's nightmare") and "spectacular, patriotic entry parades with flags, matched horses, and nattily attired riders." In order to attract the top competitors, the brothers offered big money prizes, as well as increasingly exotic exhibition acts, like a Brahma bull jumping over a roadster.

On the upside, for the Cowboys' Reunion rodeo, the Beutler brothers themselves attracted contestants and exhibition acts from Texas, Oklahoma, and Kansas, as well as throughout New Mexico. Their presence spread the revived rodeo's reputation and brought in the crowds, thereby increasing revenues. But this increased attention to the rodeo also changed the culture of the Cowboys' Reunion by overshadowing the dances, barbecues, and well-loved "get-togetherness." Additionally, the increased fees to cover larger prizes and attract traveling contestants reduced the number of local and working cowhands.

This was a new generation of rodeo cowboy and cowgirl, increasing the variety and thrill level of events and exhibitions. The reunion edition of the *Optic* for 1947 ran a photograph of Virginia Reger, famous trick rider, "shown show jumping her horse over an automobile. A trick she promises to perform at the Reunion rodeo." The newspaper also noted that Buddy Reger and his trick mule, Rabbit, would be performing.

Whereas in the early days of the Cowboys' Reunion, traveling to roundups was done for the good times, by the 1940s, as cowhands specialized in rodeoing, the trip needed to be cost-effective. Fredriksson points out that "when asked whether he was going to the Cheyenne Frontier Days [in] one of those early years, steer roper Ike Rude of Buffalo, Oklahoma, replied, 'Cheyenne? Hell, yes! I'd go there just to hear the band play.'" But by the mid-1940s, Rude was number one in the steer roping standings, and in order to make a living and maintain his standing, he had "to pursue rodeo as a career and a profession" and, therefore, be more discriminating in his travel choices. Ultimately, at age fifty-nine, Rude "roped" the World Champion title.

In the first phase, the Cowboys' Reunion rodeo had been well respected for its "square deal" approach in an era that misled and cheated the contestants, and it had maintained its status as a regional, working-cowhand and rancher roundup. If the revived reunion and rodeo hoped to stay afloat in the new competitive sport that had once been "the play of the working cowboy," it would need to keep up with the times. The 1948 rodeo program listed, in place of the Legion's rodeo committee, the Cowboys' Reunion and Rodeo Association (CRRA), with officers, directors, and ex-officio members representing various civic clubs. This association is sometimes listed in programs or mentioned in newspaper coverage, but unlike its predecessor, the Cowboys' Reunion Association of 1915, it is not registered as a for-profit corporation. The members of the association worked as volunteers, gathering more volunteers to make sure that the rodeo portion happened without a hitch. They did everything from cleaning up and repairing the grounds to registering contestants and stock, hiring rodeo production staff, promoting activities, keeping time, arranging for judges, and providing awards. At the close of the three-day event, the CRRA settled the dust and made financial reports to the community.

A brief article entitled "The Untold Story…" in the 1950 rodeo souvenir program thanked the people and organizations of Las Vegas that helped put on each reunion, indicating the extent to which the organizational structure of the Cowboys' Reunion was changing:

> *The advertisers in this book are part of the group. The official Cowboys' Reunion band is another. The service clubs and civic organizations in*

> *Las Vegas have contributed assistance too plentiful to detail completely. Ranchers and stockmen, the Mounted Patrol, Sheriff's Posse, the mounted Square Dance Club, all have been unselfish in cooperation. Housewives mailed out Reunion Booster postal cards.*

The program also mentioned the help of Highlands University, the Civil Air Patrol's "breakfast flight" for pilots, the Las Vegas–San Miguel Chamber of Commerce, the fine rodeo stock, and the "hundreds who did their part by wearing western togs." The article was signed "the Cowboys of the Southwest." Previously, the 1941 rodeo program had credited an additional source of community support, the *Optic*, which provided "unbuyable publicity."

The American Legion Cowboys' Reunion was gathering momentum just as the country was entering another recession and northeastern New Mexico was experiencing severe drought. The issues of the 1950s strained finances and once again threatened the ranching way of life. Throughout the revival period, the local community provided much support, but as economic ups and downs continued and people's entertainment desires changed, attendance at large-scale, multiple-day events like the Cowboys' Reunion began falling off. However, Las Vegans pulled together again. Local ranchers and businesses, service clubs, and the Las Vegas–San Miguel Chamber of Commerce joined the American Legion to help with the many aspects of the reunion. These groups provided promotional and booster activities, sponsored individual events, and expanded the much-needed volunteer base.

During the late 1940s, as part of the overall publicity campaign, Cowboys' Reunion rodeo programs and local media began emphasizing a relationship between the Cowboys' Reunion and the Roosevelt's Rough Riders encampments, which took place in various parts of the country to commemorate the Battle of Las Guasimas in Cuba. The first Rough Rider encampment, officially titled the First Annual Reunion Roosevelt's Rough Riders, took place on June 24–26, 1899, in Las Vegas, and Theodore Roosevelt attended. In 1949, the Rough Riders returned to Las Vegas for a Golden Jubilee in June, and by August, the Cowboys' Reunion rodeo program pictured Theodore Roosevelt on its cover and referred to the Cowboys' Reunion as "the off spring of the famous Rough Riders." This connection had been suggested in earlier Cowboys' Reunion literature, and the two events continue to be confused. However, in 1952, the Roosevelt's Rough Rider Association did indeed combine its annual encampment with the Fourteenth Annual Las Vegas Cowboys' Reunion.

"The Granddaddy of Them All,"
1952–1968

Outstanding on New Mexico's summer calendar is the big twin event in Las Vegas on August 7, 8 and 9—The Annual Cowboys' Reunion and the annual Teddy Roosevelt Rough Riders Encampment.
—New Mexico Magazine

In 1952, enticed by the local chamber of commerce and area ranchers—specifically James W. Arrott—the Roosevelt's Rough Rider Reunion Association (RRR) changed its traditional encampment dates and met in Las Vegas during Cowboys' Reunion days. Additionally, at that year's annual meeting, RRR members voted to hold all subsequent reunion encampments in Las Vegas during the Cowboys' Reunion until the last veteran could no longer attend. How this union of two reunions came about is part of the story of the endurance of the Cowboys' Reunion and the perseverance of Las Vegans.

In a letter to Robert W. Denny of the RRR, Arrott approached the association with two proposals: one, that the 1952 reunion be held in Las Vegas during the Cowboys' Reunion; and two, that the RRR make the Las Vegas Cowboys' Reunion its annual reunion destination:

> *Since your first Reunion [1899] was held in Las Vegas, New Mexico and you have decided to have a Reunion each year until no one can attend, then I think you could consider holding all your future Reunions in Las Vegas until the last man is gone. In this way your members could get used to the location, could look forward to the same town each year to gather for their Reunion, and I believe this arrangement would result in a larger attendance.*

Arrott's letter made a strong case for the benefits of a permanent home for the annual Rough Rider encampment and offered the support of the Las Vegas–San Miguel Chamber of Commerce through its secretary, Louis (also spelled Lewis) F. Schiele. As further enticement, Arrott pointed out the logistical benefit—railway transportation—and offered discounts on Las Vegas accommodations.

However, the merger was not as simple or as logical as it might first appear. For the RRR, a motion would need to be made and approved at the annual membership meeting, establishing the new location and changing the encampment dates to coincide with those of the Cowboys' Reunion. For the Cowboys' Reunion, the chamber of commerce would need to secure the approval of all Cowboys' Reunion sponsors as well as the Cowboys' Reunion and Rodeo Association; the name of the event would need to change to include the First United States Volunteer Cavalry; and the Cowboys' Reunion management would need to establish a committee dedicated to handling all the specific needs of the Rough Riders and their families.

In spite of the difficulties, Arrott was successful. In a June 10, 1952 letter to Rough Rider colonel Martin Crimmins, Arrott explained, "It has been definitely decided that the National Association of Roosevelt's Rough Riders will hold its 1952 Reunion in Las Vegas on August 1st, 2nd, and 3rd…At this same time the Annual Las Vegas Cowboy's Reunion is being held and it is the intent that both Reunions will be held together."

Thus, the first part of Arrott's proposal succeeded, but he made it clear that it took some doing to secure the agreement of deciding members Robert Denny, Billy McGinty, and Jesse Langdon, the chair of the Reunion Committee: "After considerable delay and after the [Rough Riders] Reunion being first on, and then off, Mr. Langdon has just approved the dates," confirming that the Rough Riders would meet in reunion at Las Vegas during the annual Cowboys' Reunion of 1952.

At this point in the process, in another letter to Crimmins, Arrott adopted the notion, already established in much of the Cowboys' Reunion publicity, that the "Las Vegas Cowboy's Reunion is the outgrowth of the Rough Rider's Reunion in 1898 [*sic*]." This artificial relationship between the two reunions has held fast, being touted in a variety of public announcements, newspaper and magazine articles, Cowboys' Reunion rodeo programs, local histories, and in the hearts and minds of those who recall attending the combined Rough Riders and Cowboys' Reunions beginning in 1952. The source of this tenuous connection may be traced to a reference used in a 1915 "pre-rodeo announcement" as quoted in the article "Return of the Rough Riders" by Walter Vivian:

> *For the first time since Col. Theodore Roosevelt held the Reunion of his famous Rough Riders, back in '99, Las Vegas is to be the meeting place for the Cowboys of New Mexico who will again be able to talk over the days of yore when they were lads of the range, and to renew acquaintances which were formed back in the stirring times of the real West.*

Vivian went on to connect the two events by noting their similarities. Many of the veterans came from southwestern ranching and cowboy culture, and both events were focused on "re-uniting." But the Cowboys' Reunion Association and related records and rodeo programs do not indicate an organizational relationship between the two associations or their reunions until 1952.

Arrott was correct, however, in arguing that the combined reunions would result in larger attendance for both the Rough Riders and the Cowboys' Reunion audiences. As promised, the community gathered its resources to honor the veterans and sustain the annual celebration of ranching culture. With an annual destination point established for the Rough Riders, travel and accommodation discounts were offered.

Arrott's ultimate appeal was to the pride of the veterans. In a letter to Colonel Crimmins, Arrott brought up a competition between Cheyenne, Wyoming, and Las Vegas, New Mexico, stating that the Rough Riders' first reunion predated Frontier Days: "As you know their posters and advertising always says that the Frontier Days in Cheyenne is, 'The Daddy of them all.' I think we have a right to call ours the Grand-Daddy as you men started the first one and that was a couple of years before the Frontier Days started in Cheyenne." Although Arrott is mistaken about the origins of these events—Cheyenne Frontier Days began in 1897, two years before the first RRR encampment of 1899—his motives and those of the Cowboys' Reunion organizers and sponsors indicate a strong commitment to securing and sustaining both events.

The outcome of Arrott's proposals was reported in the June 23, 1952 edition of the *Optic*, which noted that the Roosevelt's Rough Rider Association would hold its 1952 reunion in Las Vegas at the same time as the Cowboys' Reunion, "at which time the proposal to make Las Vegas the permanent site for annual encampments will be brought before the group." At this point, the Cowboys' Reunion rodeo committee renamed the 1952 event as the "Rough Riders–Cowboys [sic] Reunion." On August 3, 1952, during its annual meeting, the RRR named Las Vegas its permanent meeting place for all future encampments and determined that its reunions would be held "in conjunction with the Cowboys' Reunion the first Friday, Saturday and Sunday in August."

The 1952 combined reunions garnered national media attention, bringing *Life* magazine photographer George Kew, who shot memorable photographs of the veterans and the community that honored them. The August 25 issue of *Life* carried a three-page spread with photos of Rough Riders Billy McGinty and Jesse Langdon on horseback leading the Cowboys' Reunion parade down Douglas Avenue, as well as a shot of Diana Sandefer (also spelled Sandifer), that year's rodeo queen, and Langdon kicking up their heels at a western dance. Unfortunately, the brief article does not mention the Cowboys' Reunion and its role in hosting the veterans.

The Rough Riders added their own special brand of "ballyhoo" to the Cowboys' Reunion. For fourteen years, they came from all over the country and brought their wives and extended families. They appeared in the parades and at the rodeos, sometimes on horseback. Some veterans sported cowboy togs—angora chaps, big Stetsons, flamboyant shirts, and the ever-present neckerchief—while others proudly wore their uniforms. The veterans filled the rodeo grandstands and occupied the hotels. The Castañeda, where Roosevelt himself had stayed in 1899, and El Fidel, close to the railway depot, were favorites. The men truly "re-unioned," gathering in lobbies and at luncheons to recollect and get reacquainted. Several of the Rough Riders composed and presented memoirs written especially for these reunions.

According to the June 28 *Optic*, for the combined reunion rodeo of 1952 the American Legion rodeo committee announced an additional event, "Big Steer Roping," with a $100 entry fee and a $500 purse. Committee member Dee Bibb stated that steer roping "separates the men from the boys." That year and the following year, Tommy Steiner of the Steiner Rodeo Company, a professional contractor out of Austin, Texas, produced the rodeo. "Steiner rodeos were known for elaborate grand entries, fast colorful productions, beautiful parade horses, and the finest equipment and stock," continuing the excitement and spectacle of the previous Beutler brothers' productions.

The community and area ranchers extended a hearty welcome to the Rough Riders. The *Optic* ran stories about the Spanish-American War and the individual veterans, and based on City of Las Vegas Museum documents, Ernie Thwaites organized and produced several radio shows and remote transmissions from KFUN Radio. In 1952, a color guard of Rough Riders led the reunion parade and the rodeo's Grand Entry. Rough Rider veterans and their families attended rodeo sessions, square-danced at the Castañeda Ballroom, spent "A Day in the Country" at the Arrott Ranch, and toured Fort Union, which did not become a national monument until 1956. The Santa Fe Railway Company joined the celebratory events by hosting a banquet to honor the veterans. In a letter to Barron Bashoar of *Time* magazine, Arrott declared the 1952 combined reunion event "a howling success. We had twenty-nine

Cowboys and Rough Riders. Cowboys' Reunion Rodeo Grand Entry, 1953. *From front to back*: Rough Riders Billy McGinty, Jesse Langdon, Charles Hopping, Dick Shanafelt and Arthur Tuttle. Note the chaps, or leggings, on McGinty. Worn by working cowboys for protection, chaps were usually leather. These angoras were made from goatskin, leaving the hair long for warmth. *Courtesy City of Las Vegas Museum and Rough Rider Memorial Collection, 2011.2.543.*

Rough Riders, of which six were also Buffalo Bill Wild West Show men and the old gentlemen certainly had the time of their life."

The following year, 1953, marked the first officially sanctioned—that is, approved by the RRR membership—combined Cowboys' and Rough Riders Reunion. Las Vegas was as high-spirited as a colt on spring grass. A six-page spread in the *Optic* described the luncheons, rodeo, square dancing exhibitions by the Las Vegas Twirlers, the parade, cakewalks, street dances, invited guests, and, of course, personal stories that characterized the 1953 celebrations. The Rough Riders were especially appreciative of the Native American dance troupe that traveled from Taos, New Mexico, to entertain them.

Personal stories of reunion experiences during the 1950s and '60s are still circulated throughout Las Vegas. At the "Teatime with the Old-Timers" gathering on August 1, 2006, Petey Salmon told the story of how she did not become rodeo queen for the year 1953. Leo Montoya, of Leo's Glass and Glazing, challenged Petey, a Las Vegas "town girl," to run against Joan Shoemaker, a working cowgirl. Well, Petey had

ROOSEVELT'S ROUGH RIDERS AND THE COWBOYS' REUNION
(GRANDDADDY OF 'EM ALL)
LAS VEGAS, NEW MEXICO, AUGUST 7, 8, 9, 1953

COLORFUL ROUGH RIDERS WHO MEET ANNUALLY IN LAS VEGAS TO THE "LAST MAN" PLUS ONE OF THE LEADING RODEOS IN THE WORLD

Prizes $500 in Each of Five Major Events (All Entry Fees Added)

"STAY WITH 'IM"
STOCK FURNISHED BY DON GILMORE

In 1952, Roosevelt's Rough Riders partnered up with Cowboys' Reunion "until the last man," doubling the appeal. Together, the annual gatherings continued for another sixteen years. *Courtesy City of Las Vegas Museum and Rough Rider Memorial Collection, 102.12.20.*

never done much riding, but she got into the spirit of things and rode a borrowed mount, Buttons, in the parade. When one of the Rough Rider veterans blew his bugle, Buttons bolted. Clearly, Salmon and Buttons would not win the horsemanship aspect of the competition. Shoemaker was crowned rodeo queen. The reunion rodeo queens provided much publicity and served as countrywide goodwill ambassadors. In 1953, the previous year's queen, Diana Sandefer, of the Dead Horse Ranch near Las Vegas, made the cover of *New Mexico Magazine*, and as "one of the Madison Square Garden Rodeo queens representing New Mexico," she publicized her hometown.

In subsequent years, although primarily honored at the Cowboys' Reunion rodeo, the visiting veterans were also romanced by area ranchers such as James Arrott and Gib Sandefer and by politicians. Patrick Hurley, former secretary of war, ambassador to China, and minister to New Zealand, hosted luncheons for the Rough Riders, who made him an honorary member of the RRR. Even so, the old gentlemen always made time to congregate in Las Vegas hotel lobbies and kick up their heels at the dances.

Throughout the 1950s and '60s, in addition to the presence of the Rough Riders, the Cowboys' Reunion organizers hosted several activities that kept the event in the public eye and increased attendance. At the same time, rodeo in general gained increasing national attention and continued moving toward the professional sport it would become. In Las Vegas, the Cowboys' Reunion and its rodeo sometimes struggled to find a balance between financial growth and mission while, at the same time, sustaining itself financially as part of the rodeo world. On July 3, 1954, the *Optic* reported:

> *Rodeo fans have grown to expect the best in performances at the Cowboys' Reunion rodeo which has a national rating with the better rodeo performances. Champions in all classes have been seen in the arena at the Legion rodeo plant on North Seventh street.*
>
> *Contestants and performers have conceded that they are "always treated right in Vegas" and are ready to return in the future.*

Although the three-day event was experiencing growing pains, organizers continued to offer quality dance bands, dinners and barbecues, and the annual parade. To its credit, Las Vegas never forgot its reunion days' priorities. The following announcement appeared on the front page of the *Optic* on August 6, 1953:

> HORSES GET GREEN LIGHT
>
> *Horses have the right-of-way.*
> *That's the orders of Chief Matt E. O'Brien of the city police.*
> *"During the Rough Riders–Cowboys' Reunion, there will be a lot of people on horseback and some of the horses will be flighty. We want to give the horsemen a break, so if motorists will be careful in passing horses it will be appreciated."*

The dances and especially the dance bands continued to be a major attraction, sometimes garnering better receipts than the rodeo. One of the most popular dance bands, coming back year after year, was Dick Bills & the Sandia Mountain Boys. In Las Vegas, a story has circulated that Glen

Campbell performed at the Castañeda Hotel. Well, it may very likely be true. From 1954 to 1955, Campbell, in his teen years, played guitar and toured with his uncle, Dick Bills. According to the *Optic* of August 4, Dick Bills & the Sandia Mountain Boys performed at the crowning of the 1955 Cowboys' Reunion rodeo queen at the Castañeda Hotel. Other popular reunion orchestras of this era included the Elton Travis Band and the Clayton Troubadours. At "Teatime with the Old-Timers," the names of two additional bands came up: Tommy Hines's Westernaires from Los Alamos and the Heastonaires.

In 1955, the Cowboys' Reunion enjoyed the reign of two queens. No, it was not a tie for rodeo queen. The rodeo elected as its queen Gordy Maxine Thatcher, who was crowned by NBC's television queen Ruth Lutz. Lutz had won a trip on *Queen for a Day* to be the guest of Las Vegas throughout the three-day event. Like the Rough Riders, Lutz and her husband arrived in Las Vegas by rail and attended the rodeo sessions. Mrs. Lutz was the guest of honor at banquets and luncheons sponsored by various social clubs, and she rode in a vehicle in the parade. That year, eighteen veterans and their family members attended. Maintaining the high spirits of the event, the *Optic* reported, "Romping on schedule the three-day 17th annual Cowboys' Reunion and 56th annual Roosevelt [sic] Rough Riders encampment went into its first day today with a full program of related activities which will be wound up with the final rodeo Sunday afternoon."

As tradition dictated, and even though the route often changed, everything started off with "a mile long parade." According to the *Optic*:

> *The parade started from Hot Springs Boulevard and wended its way through Greater Las Vegas over spectator-lined streets.*
>
> *Paced by Charles O'Malley, parade marshall [sic] who was aided by the 20-30 club, the parade featured over 100 mounted riders.*

The 20-30 Club was one of many social and civic organizations that partnered up to sponsor the dual reunions.

The 1956 Rough Riders and Cowboys' Reunion again enjoyed the national spotlight when Major General Harry Reichelderfer attended as representative of President Dwight D. Eisenhower and accepted a plaque from the Las Guasimas veterans naming Eisenhower an honorary colonel of the First United States Volunteer Cavalry. The award ceremony took place at the Arrott Ranch, Sapello, New Mexico, further embellishing the appeal of reunion time in Las Vegas.

Even before these events put the Rough Riders and Cowboys' Reunion in the spotlight, the annual celebrations had grown into one huge affair, and members of the Legion's Rodeo Association were feeling like a green cowpoke on a sunfishing bronc. In 1953, the Legion entertained the possibility

Cowboys and aliens, a sign of the times, in 1953, Bridge Street at Twelfth Street. *Courtesy City of Las Vegas Museum and Rough Rider Memorial Collection, 2011.2.537.*

of giving up sponsorship of the annual event. In a 1954 *Optic* article, W.R. "Shy" Sheihagen, president of the Cowboys' Reunion Rodeo Committee, explained that although the Legion continued to support the reunion, it is "a Greater Las Vegas undertaking," and other organizations were needed to help with promotion and operational details. In a 1958 article for *New Mexico Magazine*, Vivian described how the community pulled together in the "get-togetherness" spirit of reunion:

> *It was agreed to expand the rodeo committee to take in the Legion, Rotary, Kiwanis, Elks, Chamber of Commerce and Jaycees representatives. Two members from each organization, plus appointive rancher members, were named to take over the details. An enlarged rodeo plant is next on the program. The stands are just not big enough.*

This reorganization helped accommodate the additional needs of the RRR as well as the burgeoning requirements of putting on an event that was growing by leaps and bounds. The days of the Beutler Brothers Company and the Steiner Rodeo Company brought widespread attention to the Las Vegas event. These rodeo producers had succeeded in bringing in professionally skilled rodeo athletes for big prize money and, therefore, groomed the Cowboys' Reunion rodeo into a top-notch event. However, the higher entry fees reduced the number of local working cowhands who were able to enter the contests.

Throughout the '50s and early '60s, the CRRA handled all aspects of putting on the rodeo. A number of arena directors and stock providers helped produce the rodeo, but it was the CRRA that pulled it all together. In 1960, the association contracted with Jim Shoulders, five-time all-around champion cowboy and Pro Rodeo Hall of Famer, to produce the rodeo, participate in events, and furnish the stock. The 1960 rodeo program and the *Optic* provided big spreads with a biography and photograph of Shoulders with his horse. "Shy" Scheihagen, CRRA president, said, "We are proud of the fact that the Champion of Champions is producing our rodeo this year, and he will be here in person." There are many people in Las Vegas today who proudly recall when Jim Shoulders came to town. He still holds the record for earning the most World Rodeo titles, sixteen in all.

The year 1960 also brought international rodeo contestant Grahame Fenton of Australia to compete in the saddle bronc-riding event. The *Optic* reported that Fenton would ride in "the Australian Buck-Jumping manner which includes riding a bucking horse on an Australian saddle while popping a whip. The Australian saddle is about the same size as the English postage stamp saddle."

Although Shoulders's appearance was a highlight of that year's rodeo and helped continue community-wide efforts to make the rodeo bigger and better, there were problems. On a national level, times were changing again. America was entering a period of doubt and questioning, especially related to "the establishment" (which could be interpreted in many ways) and its leadership methods. Questions arose regarding the status of the rodeo, and the tension between professional sport and working cowboy roundup increased, resulting in another turning point for the Cowboys' Reunion.

In a letter from Ozella Todhunter, longtime committee member for the Rough Riders aspect of the reunion, to Rough Rider Frank S. Roberts, Todhunter claimed that the rodeo association had paid too much money for "outside talent and stock" and noted that the 1961 rodeo "will be local men and boys and girls" showing off their talents. Todhunter also stated that the rodeo association had been re-formed. Although the rodeo association officers did change sometime before the 1961 reunion, further documentation is not available at the time of this writing.

By June 1961, Boone Stokes was president, and the CRRA, as with most new leadership, was following a different path, one that aimed to increase the number of local contestants. In the *Optic*, Stokes announced that advanced ticket sales and event registration for local entries would begin on July 27. The announcement also identified the rodeo as an amateur production, an important distinction since the establishment of the National Finals Rodeo Commission in 1958: "Rodeo headquarters have been set up at the Castañeda Hotel and that all local men and boys interested in entering this year's amateur rodeo should do so immediately. The books are open and the association would like a lot of local entries." Stokes served as rodeo association president for the 1961 and '62 reunion rodeos. In 1962, the Rough Riders and Cowboys' Reunion dates were changed; from '62 through '64, it was held in mid-June, and from 1965 to 1967, it was held during the Fourth of July Old Town Fiesta.

In 1963, Cowboys' Reunion and Rodeo Association president, George M. "Dogie" Jones, son of "Butch" Jones, one of the founding members of the 1915 Cowboys' Reunion Association, directed the rodeo and continued the strong trend toward increased inclusion of local contestants. Jones recollected that the rodeo association members recognized that professional rodeo producers had concentrated on attracting top-notch competitors, leaving little room for the local, working cowhands and ranchers. Meanwhile, on

Cowboys' Reunion rodeo winners, 1963. *From left to right*: Rex Morgan, Troy Triplet, Ronney Jackson, Jim Young (Las Vegas), Linda Post (Las Vegas), Loretta Claunch, Bill Zimmerman, Jerry Dean, Noman Palmer and association president Dogie Jones. Down in front is Jacque Mae Jones. *Courtesy George M. "Dogie" Jones Private Collection. Photo credit: Magill.*

the national level, rodeo had become big business, leaving the future of the ranch rodeos and frontier celebrations in the chute, so to speak.

In Las Vegas, in spite of venue and scheduling issues, the Cowboy's Reunion rolled along. In 1965, according to a letter from Frank C. Norris, Las Vegas–San Miguel Chamber of Commerce, to Marie Oates, the Rough Riders' attending nurse, the Cowboys' Reunion rodeo would not be held during the first weekend in August because of a conflict with the Travel Trailer Club of America Rally, a national event to be held in Las Vegas. However, that year, the Rough Riders were invited to hold their reunion as scheduled. Based on a subsequent exchange of letters between Norris and Oates, the combined Rough Riders and Cowboys' Reunion rodeo resurfaced in 1966, sponsored by Troop 3 of the Mounted Patrol, but it was rescheduled again and coincided with the Las Vegas Fourth of July Fiestas—a longstanding, three-day celebration at the Old Town Plaza Park.

The *Optic* special edition of July 1–6, 1965, filled in a few gaps for this turning point in the story of the Cowboys' Reunion: "For the first time in recent years the Cowboys Reunion Rodeo and the West Las Vegas Fiesta will be held together." In the early days of the reunion, from 1915 to 1931, the two events were both scheduled for the Fourth of July weekend, and according to the *Optic* article, "Citizens of both communities joined together to make the Fourth of July the high spot of the year in Las Vegas, and people came from all over the United States to attend the events here." Although the events were scheduled during the same time period, activities were handled by separate groups: the Fiesta Committee and the Cowboys' Reunion and Rodeo Committee. The rodeo was sponsored by Mounted Patrol Troop 3. "Shy" Scheihagen—assisted by a steering committee of Ray Crespin, Earl Manlove, Pete Ortiz, and James Leger—handled the arrangements for the four-day Cowboys' Reunion rodeo. The Rough Riders did not attend.

In 1966 and 1967, Troop 3 sponsored the rodeo that took place simultaneously with the Fourth of July Fiesta. For the Rough Riders, Jesse Langdon attended. The *Optic* announced, "Here it is folks—the first day of the 1967 edition of the Cowboys and Teddy Roosevelt Rough Riders Reunion and Rodeo and Old Town Fiesta." Throughout the final two years, the official rodeo program titled the event the "Cowboys and Roosevelt Rough Riders Reunion Rodeo." Community sponsors and businesses offered a variety of western dances and entertainment. Similar Fiesta activities took place as well, generally in the plaza area. The 1966 and '67 rodeo programs, respectively, numbered the rodeos as the twenty-eighth and twenty-ninth, linking the rodeo to the American Legion revival that began in 1939.

Optic newspaper advertisements of 1967 promised a "Big Rodeo–Fiesta Parade," dances for the rodeo at the old armory, dances for the Fiesta at

Palms Hall. The ads also declared that there would be family entertainment and three days of rodeo events at Legion Park. The day-after report announced that $2,500 in cash had been awarded to contestants, and Scheihagen, rodeo announcer and chairman, stated that "the event was a success in both the dances and the attendance at the rodeo," although he pointed out that the grandstands were not filled on the first day of the rodeo. Scheihagen served the Cowboys' Reunion in many capacities during nine of its final twelve years.

On July 7, 1967, the *Optic* reported that the rodeo had finished in the black. "Expenses for the rodeo amounted to $3,252 while receipts were $3,508.89, so that instead of going in the hole, the sponsors showed a bit of money ahead." The brief article credited the support of the local business community with its generous donations "in one way or another" for the positive financial outcome.

As the days of the Rough Rider veterans came to a close, so too did those of the Cowboys' Reunion. Rough Rider Memorial Collection correspondence and photographs indicate that Frank C. Brito and Jesse Langdon may have met in Las Vegas in 1965 but not as part of the Cowboys' Reunion. The *Optic* of 1967 and '68 noted that Jesse Langdon made the pilgrimage alone, the sole Rough Rider, and that Langdon and his family were honored at the Fiestas.

During each summer since 1952, the veterans had been honored and accommodated in Las Vegas; ceremoniously recognized at the Cowboys' Reunion rodeos, banquets, and parades; celebrated by New Mexico ranchers and *politicos*; and, in general, treated like the heroes they were. In turn, the presence of the Rough Riders helped draw national attention to the Cowboys' Reunion and to Las Vegas.

Another result of the collaboration between the RRR and the Cowboys' Reunion was a collection of artifacts and memoirs that became the foundation of a city historical museum. City of Las Vegas Museum records show that beginning with the 1952 combined reunion, several Rough Riders and their families put together a collection of mementos and photographs; in addition, and specifically for their reunions in Las Vegas, the Rough Riders wrote and collected a series of memoirs. They designated Ozella Love Todhunter, the wife of Rough Rider William Love of Las Vegas, as custodian. In 1960, the City of Las Vegas Council approved and funded a museum ordinance, and in 1961, the mayor, Leroy S. Wicks, appointed a museum board. Subsequently, Mrs. Todhunter approved a contract making the collection, after a two-year exhibit showing, the property of the City of Las Vegas. In the fall of 1963, the exhibit and the entire collection was deeded to the city and formed the basis of the City of Las Vegas Museum and Rough Rider Memorial

Collection. In this way, the Cowboys' Reunion helped provide Las Vegas with another opportunity for development.

In spite of community-wide efforts, attendance at the Cowboys' Reunions had begun falling off since the middle of the twentieth century. The August 8, 1955 *Optic* reported that "the stands were not packed at any of the [rodeo] showings." Again, in the August 7, 1961 *Optic*, then CRRA president L.L. "Boone" Stokes admitted that "the grandstands weren't full every [rodeo] performance," but the reunion ended up in the black because of ticket sales and proceeds from three dances. The CRRA and its many volunteers worked hard to support the burgeoning needs of producing a three- to four-day, large-scale event by uniting with Roosevelt's Rough Riders, garnering national attention, and bringing in famous rodeo producers and champions. However, according to Perrigo, "[I]n 1967, the deterioration of the old rodeo pavilion and the exhaustion of leadership led to the termination of the once great annual professional rodeos [in Las Vegas]."

However, the Cowboys' Reunion was not, at its core, a professional rodeo. It was a rodeo and more. It was a reunion of like-minded folks and a rodeo in the sense of "the play of the working cowboy." As American rodeo evolved, the Cowboys' Reunion rodeo stretched toward professional level by attracting rodeo athletes as well as homegrown working cowhands. For close to half a century, the Cowboys' Reunion provided a way for ranchers to get together and "neighbor" again. It drew artists and writers of all genres and provided countless subjects for their creative efforts. For the two communities that made up Las Vegas, the annual reunion and rodeo brought new visitors and increased financial input, and for a while, big-time competitors and working cowgirls and cowboys rode side by side.

The Las Vegas Cowboys' Reunion

A Retrospective

In 1984, several local organizations attempted to "resurrect" the Cowboys' Reunion. Many people worked many hours, securing the sponsorship of the Greater Las Vegas New Mexico Fiesta Committee, the Rough Riders Museum, the Sapello Rough Riders Rodeo Association, the Jr. Jaycees, the Hispano Chamber of Commerce, and Creative Printers Inc. The event took place from August 17 to April 19 and provided a banquet, a rodeo, a western dance, a barbecue, a talent show, and a street dance. Posters billed it as "Ressurrection [*sic*] of The Cowboys' Reunion." While indoor activities took place at the Castañeda Hotel facilities, the rodeo location is listed as having been at "Hot Springs Boulevard," indicating that it may have taken place at what is now the San Miguel County Fairgrounds. The three-day event had all the makings of the Cowboys' Reunion, and it was repeated for at least two additional years.

Today, there are no physical traces of Gallinas Park, the two Cowboys' Reunion Parks, or the Legion Park Rodeo Grounds. Las Vegas supports several annual parades for school and college homecoming activities and the Fourth of July, and many horses and riders join the pageant, a ghostly remnant of the Cowboys' Reunion days. There are, of course, dances and rodeos sponsored by local organizations, such as Ride to Pride and the New Mexico Highlands Rodeo Club. In addition, Las Vegas is home to Zamora Roping Productions and the Santa Fe Event Center, a first-class equine facility, hosting all types of rodeos and large-venue events.

Beginning with the first Cowboys' Reunion of 1915, each summer, Las Vegas burgeoned with the "Wild West crowd." The Great Depression dampened its dust, but in 1939, the Leonard Hoskins Post

Left: A 1917 official souvenir program and prize list. *Courtesy City of Las Vegas Museum and Rough Rider Memorial Collection, 73.16.34.*

Opposite, top left: A 1922 official daily program. *Courtesy City of Las Vegas Museum and Rough Rider Memorial Collection, 74.16.69.*

Opposite, top right: The 1939 American Legion First Annual Cowboys' Reunion. *Courtesy City of Las Vegas Museum and Rough Rider Memorial Collection, 73.16.82.*

Opposite, bottom: The 1948 Annual Cowboys' Reunion souvenir program. *Courtesy City of Las Vegas Museum and Rough Rider Memorial Collection, 73.16.90.*

Above, left: The 1950 Cowboys' Reunion program, the only cover with a female bronc rider. *Courtesy City of Las Vegas Museum and Rough Rider Memorial Collection, 73.16.92.*

Above, right: The 1953 Roosevelt's Rough Riders and Cowboy's Reunion program. In 1952, the Rough Rider Association joined the cowboys for a dual reunion and voted to hold all subsequent encampments during the Las Vegas Cowboys' Reunion. *Courtesy City of Las Vegas Museum and Rough Rider Memorial Collection, 73.16.95.*

Left: The 1959 cover, featuring cowboys and rodeo contests. *Courtesy City of Las Vegas Museum and Rough Rider Memorial Collection, 73.16.101.*

A 1962 rodeo action shot. Cowboys' and Roosevelt Rough Riders Reunion rodeo. *Courtesy George M. "Dogie" Jones Private Collection.*

A 1963 graphic design, with addition of calf roping. *Courtesy George M. "Dogie" Jones Private Collection.*

Saddle bronc riding, 1964, featuring the artwork of Robert K. Abbett. *Courtesy City of Las Vegas Museum and Rough Rider Memorial Collection, 2012.1.1.*

of the American Legion got it going again. Wars, recessions, and natural disasters threatened the reunions, but with the help of civic groups, Las Vegas merchants, Roosevelt's Rough Riders, the Cowboys' Reunion and Rodeo Association, and the New Mexico Mounted Patrol Troop 3, Las Vegas kept the Cowboys' Reunion and its rodeo going until 1967.

Although rodeo was a large part of the big event, the balls, carnivals, parades, big-name bands, western dances, barbecues, fancy suppers, and especially the opportunities for getting reacquainted were just as important. It is true that the Las Vegas business community was instrumental in supporting and developing the Cowboys' Reunion at Las Vegas, but the area ranchers and cowhands were the prime moving forces. With their "Git Fer Vegas" attitudes, these men and women made the Cowboys' Reunions and rodeos happen and happen big. Through boom and bust, the annual Las Vegas Cowboys' Reunion spanned several generations and survived wars, nationwide financial woes, political assassinations, droughts, major challenges to the American ranching and cowhand culture, and the constantly evolving world of rodeo. The story of the Cowboys' Reunion is a story of endurance and adaptation, a story that reflects the history of Las Vegas itself.

The Git Fer Vegas, Cowboy! Exhibit

It all began with the daily work of the museum. In the summer of 2008, I began to catalogue—that is, create records for items in the collection. I began assembling and organizing a large group of documents including letters, rodeo programs, assorted publications, newspaper clippings, receipts, notes, and photographs that were somehow related to something called the Cowboys' Reunion or the Rough Riders Reunion or both. By examining the museum's Rough Rider Memorial Collection, I realized that the two reunions were separate events, and I was able to sort the papers and photographs into a general category—Cowboys' Reunion—and categorize the items chronologically. During the months of sorting and classifying items and as I researched the historical context, I came to understand both the separation and the connections between the Rough Rider Memorial Collection and the materials related to the Las Vegas Cowboys' Reunion. Ultimately, the documents and photographs told the story of three events: the Roosevelt's Rough Rider Association Reunion, the Cowboys' Reunion, and the Roosevelt's Rough Rider and Cowboys' Reunion.

Daily, as I sorted through the Cowboys' Reunion items, they began to form a collection, and as fast as I could create records for the items, additional items surfaced. Linda, the museum director, uncovered additional documents and photographs that could be cross-referenced to the archival items on which I was working. In addition, with documents dating back to 1915, I began to realize the scope of the collection. Clearly, these materials and their story were worthy of an exhibit, and soon the exhibit developed its own momentum.

In October 2008, I learned that the New Mexico Humanities Council was sponsoring a centennial tour to commemorate the 100th anniversary of the publication of N. Howard "Jack" Thorp's premier collection of cowboy ballads, *Songs of the Cowboys*, published in Estancia, New Mexico, in 1908. The centennial tour would take the shape of period musical performances by Mark Gardner and Rex Rideout. Through my research catalogue work, I was aware that in the early 1920s, Thorp visited the Las Vegas Cowboys' Reunion, collected additional lyrics for his second edition, and composed a song, "Las Vegas Reunion." Needless to say, the museum was a perfect place to host one of the centennial performances.

However, the timing was off. The tour was already set, and Las Vegas was not on the bill. Discussions among Gardner, the museum staff, and the museum's support group, the Friends of the City of Las Vegas Museum and Rough Rider Memorial Collection ("the Friends"), convinced everyone that first, the collection was worthy of its own exhibit; second, that a collaboration with Clovis, New Mexico, also not on the tour, was a must; and third, that the *Songs of the Cowboys Centennial Concert* performance was the perfect way to open the exhibit.

In March 2009, the Friends of the City of Las Vegas Museum received a grant award from the New Mexico Humanities Council to produce a Las Vegas Cowboys' Reunion project. Additional funding was received from the Los Alamos National Laboratory Foundation, the Citizens Bank of Clovis, the Clovis Carver Public Library, and the Friends of the City of Las Vegas Museum and Rough Rider Memorial Collection. The results were an exhibit covering the Cowboys' Reunion story from 1915 to 1967 entitled Git Fer Vegas, Cowboy! and two performances of *Songs of the Cowboys*, a concert performance in tribute to N. Howard "Jack" Thorp presented by Mark Gardner and Rex Rideout—one at Clovis Carver Public Library in Clovis, New Mexico, and one in Las Vegas for the opening of the exhibit.

As guest curator, I got to hunt down and select objects to be displayed and compose the exhibit narrative and captions. As preparation, I researched the annual event and its historical context, as well as its various locations and the many people involved. The story of the Cowboys' Reunion had to fit on no more than four panels, which would also be illustrated. To say the most possible in the fewest number of words required a major honing of my writing skills.

Fortunately, I did not work in a vacuum. Experienced exhibit designer Linda Gegick pulled together the sometimes disparate artifacts that I selected and often suggested others. She identified and cleared the exhibit space and supervised all aspects of reproductions, panel design, and general display, which

The Git Fer Vegas, Cowboy! exhibit, City of Las Vegas Museum and Rough Rider Memorial Collection, from 2009 to the present. *Courtesy Edwina Portelle Romero. Photo credit: Veronica Black.*

involved constructing a wall, painting and washing floors, and arranging for proper display cases and stands. The museum educator, Nellie Price, created an interactive display, a fun way to teach rodeo's esoteric vocabulary. The artifacts themselves were a major source of help in telling the story.

And then there was the serendipitous appearance of additional Cowboys' Reunion artifacts. One of the exciting things about research is how it sends out vibrations and generates more good stuff. A few weeks before the exhibit was scheduled to open, a well-known member of the community, Bernie Allingham, loaned the museum an original 1915 Cowboys' Reunion souvenir rodeo program, and Dolores Tapia brought in a championship belt buckle belonging to her father, Ernesto Tapia, a local rancher and Cowboys' Reunion rodeo contestant from the 1940s to the '60s. Both items were part of the exhibit for two years.

As the exhibit and its story evolved and came together, it filled one of the museum galleries with saddles, Cowboys' Reunion staff items like an employee's pass and a staff shirt, orange angora chaps, enlarged photo panels of rodeo contestants from the past, documents, and souvenirs. The Las Vegas Cowboys' Reunion had come to life again.

Afterword

This book represents a pioneer study, the first full-length history of the Cowboys' Reunions at Las Vegas, New Mexico. The story spans about forty-six years of reunions and rodeos and, for the most part, was gleaned from primary sources—original photographs, official documents, original programs and schedules of events, personal and professional correspondence, newspaper accounts and advertisements, as well as personal recollections. Secondary sources—books and articles—helped provide context and perspectives.

Examination of the sources revealed, first and foremost, that the Cowboys' Reunion event was a thrilling, activity-filled "rollicky good time." Throughout the years, the various organizers maintained the event as a way for ranchers and cowhands to come together to share news, jokes, stories, and new skills—in other words, to neighbor. Activities were scheduled to provide a wide variety of good times: parades; fancy and not-so-fancy balls; lots of good food; gathering opportunities; and a traditional, working rancher-cowhand rodeo. The annual reunions spanned forty-six years and involved close to three generations.

From the sources, I compiled my best effort to reveal the complex and many-layered story of the Cowboys' Reunion from its inception in 1915 and through its booms and busts to its end circa 1967. However, this history is not comprehensive; rather, it is an overview of events. Many people's personal experiences of the reunions could not be included here. For people who want information about individual contestants, the City of Las Vegas

Afterword

Museum and Rough Rider Memorial Collection archives is the best source of information.

History is malleable. It depends on the available sources and interpretations of those sources. It depends on which documents were selected for preservation and who selected them and for what purposes. History also depends on the memories of those who lived and recorded it. Even if written in stone, the interpretations of the stonecutter determine what story is told.

As in all pioneer efforts, this book represents a beginning. As people read it, I hope it will jog memories and uncover additional stories of the big reunions and rodeos at Las Vegas. Most years, the reunions involved the entire population, from store clerks to bank tellers to homemakers, dressed in western togs and celebrating the cowhand way of life. Ultimately, all stories of the annual Cowboys' Reunion reflect the story of twentieth-century Las Vegas, New Mexico, and the story of the Southwest. I am honored to have been involved in this telling.

Appendix I

Legends and Literati

Throughout the years, the annual Cowboys' Reunion at Las Vegas attracted local, working cowhands and ranchers as well as rodeo legends, artists, writers, songwriters, poets, photographers, and filmmakers. The following are partial lists of legendary rodeo participants and well-known literati. The lists do not include local contestants, organizers and supporters because such a list would fill a separate volume.

Rodeo Legends

J.V. "Tex" Austin (1886–1938), national rodeo producer, began his career as arena director for the Cowboys' Reunion rodeos and founding board member of the first Cowboys' Reunion Association.

Frederick "Foghorn" Clancy, announcer at Cheyenne, New York, Boston, and the Las Vegas Cowboys' Reunions circa 1916–20.

Montana Belle, bronc rider, trick riding, and relay race; Cowboys' Reunions circa 1916–18.

Prairie Lillie Allen, bronc riding; Cowboys' Reunions circa 1915–17.

Prairie Rose Henderson (real name Ann Robbins, circa 1880–1939), rancher, cowgirl, bronc rider, 1916 New York City Stampede bronc-riding title winner; Cowboys' Reunions of 1917 and 1918.

Bill Stanton (died in 1921), bronc riding; Cowboys' Reunions circa 1915–21.

Mayme Saunders Stroud (died in 1963), trick rider, bronc rider, synchronized exhibition riding and chariot races; Cowboys' Reunions from about the 1920s to the 1940s.

Appendix I

William Leonard Stroud (1893–1961), rodeo champion, trick rider, Roman Races.

Clyde Lindsey, bronc riding; Cowboys' Reunions of 1916 and 1917.

Texas Annie, bull-riding exhibitions; Cowboys' Reunions circa 1915–19.

Hoyt Hefner, famous rodeo clown; Cowboys' Reunion of 1944.

Cecil Cornish and his performance horse, Smokey; Cowboys' Reunion of 1944.

Virginia Reger, trick riding; Cowboys' Reunions of the 1940s.

Jim Shoulders (1928–2007), five PRCA World All-Around Rodeo Champion Cowboys' Awards, in addition to bull riding and bareback riding awards; Cowboys' Reunion rodeo producer in 1960.

"Idaho" Bill's Famous Outlaw Horses, including Bear-Cat Blood, Hell-O-Bill, Tucumcari Lizard, Obregon, Amarillo Red Eye, Wagon Mound Horn-Toad, Harding, Owyhee, Bitter Root, Rim Rock, U-Boat, Shoshone, Powder River, Red Bird, Watrous Pussy-Foot, Gin Fiz, Vegas Belle, the Santa Fe Scorpion, Silver City, Blackfoot, the Mora Centipede, the Albuquerque Killer, Snow Ball (girls' horse) and Bolly (girls' horse); Cowboys' Reunion of 1916.

Whitmore's Bucking Horses, including Sapello King, Rocking Liz, Jazz Blue, Star Gazer, Cockeyed Pete, Snort, Loco, Roxie, Danner and Rarring Ann; Cowboys' Reunion of 1916.

Cowboys' Reunion Literati: Artists, Composers, Filmmakers, Poets, and Writers

Robert K. Abbett (born in 1926) is an American artist and illustrator specializing in outdoor scenes. One of his drawings is reproduced on the cover of the 1964 Rough Riders and Cowboys' Reunion rodeo souvenir program.

Ruth Monro Augur (1886–1967) was a painter of western America. She studied with Robert Henri in New York but was drawn to the Southwest for her subjects. Augur's illustrations appeared in an advertisement for the reunion in the *Evening Herald* of Albuquerque, New Mexico.

S. Omar Barker (1894–1985) was a New Mexican rancher, writer, and teacher. His publications include short stories, articles, publicity, poetry, and books. Some titles include

Appendix I

Vientos de las Sierras, *Buckaroo Ballads*, and *Rawhide Rhymes: Singing Poems of the Old West*. Barker was a constant presence throughout both phases of the Cowboys' Reunion.

John Edward Borein (1872–1945) was a rancher-artist and began sketching at the age of five. He is famous for his accurate depictions of the vanishing American West. Museum records indicate that Borein attended the 1921 reunion and sketched Bill Stanton's final bronc ride, "with reins in teeth." This drawing was reprinted for reunion posters and program covers.

Pascal Bozeman was a poet who composed "Hermit Lee" in 1916.

Gerald Cassidy (1879–1934) was an internationally recognized painter, featured at the Las Vegas First National Bank Building art exhibit for the 1928 reunion.

Randall Davey (1887–1964), who studied with Robert Henri in New York, often used horses as subjects in his work. The etching reproduced in this book, *Wild Horses—Cow Boys Reunion*, was created after Davey moved to Santa Fe in 1919. The image depicts a wrangler herding broncos into a corral at the Las Vegas Cowboys' Reunion rodeo.

Will James (1892–1942), author and illustrator, began sketching at the age of four and is best known for his Newberry Medal–winning book *Smoky the Cow Horse*. A postcard with LeNoir's poem "Down on the Ole Bar G," along with a sketch by Will James, was made and used as publicity for the 1924 Cowboys' Reunion.

Phil LeNoir (1882–1923), author, poet, publicist. LeNoir edited *Reunion News* and collaborated with S. Omar Barker on the short story "When Texas Annie Rode the Bull." Additional titles include *Devil's Bowl*; a movie based on his short story, "The Man Who Wouldn't Take Off His Hat"; and *Rhymes of the Wild and Woolly*, a collection of cowboy poetry.

Tom Mix (1880–1940), actor-director, made close to twenty films at the Selig Polyscope Company lot near his home on Gallinas Street in Las Vegas. Scenes in *How Weary Went Wooing* were filmed on location at the First Annual Cowboys' Reunion rodeo. Mix and the motion picture company's Daredevil Performers competed in the first reunion.

Mutual Film Company of New York filmed selected Cowboys' Reunion and rodeo events for Mutual Weekly Picture news service in 1918.

Almeron Newman (born in 1875) was known for his panoramas. Born in Deming, New Mexico, he settled in Trinidad, Colorado, in 1909. He enlisted during World War I and made many military panoramas. He produced panoramic photographs at the Cowboys' Reunions of the 1910s and 1920s.

Appendix I

J.A. Stirrat of Stirrat & Millar, Las Vegas, 1905–6, was a photographer and provided images for *Las Vegas Gallinas Park and the Scenic Highway*.

N. Howard "Jack" Thorp (1867–1940) collected cowboy song lyrics and poetry. He first published *Songs of the Cowboys* in 1908. He collected poetry and song lyrics at Cowboys' Reunion and composed "Las Vegas Reunion" for his second edition of cowboy lyrics in 1921.

Cowboys' Reunion Musicians and Orchestras

The Las Vegas Cowboys' Band, also referred to as the Cowboys' Reunion Band, had been formed by 1916 with B.J. Pattison as its first director. By the 1920s, it had grown to thirty-two musicians and was performing throughout the United States and in London, England. It was often referred to as "the most famous organization of its kind in the west."

The Simison Orchestra, 1916.

The 120 Engineers' Band, 1928.

Kasper's Band, 1928.

Dick Bills & the Sandia Mountain Boys played for Cowboys' Reunion dances throughout the 1950s and '60s.

The Melodylanders.

Ned and His Melody Busters, 1947.

Los Nativos of Santa Fe, 1947.

The Heastonaires, 1948.

Tommy Hines' Westernaires from Los Alamos, New Mexico.

The 7 Notes, 1948.

Al Thrasher and His Orchestra, 1951.

Dee Bibb and His Orchestra, 1950s.

The Elton Travis Band, 1950s and 1960s.

Appendix II
Cowboys' Reunion
A Chronology

1822: Spanish land grant of Las Vegas area, agricultural.

1835: Mexican land grant of *Nuestra Señora de los Dolores de Las Vegas*, includes village infrastructure.

1884: New Mexico territorial legislature disincorporates all municipalities, requiring them to reincorporate under new territorial rules.

1888: East Las Vegas reincorporates as the City of Las Vegas.

June 24–26, 1899: Las Vegas hosts the First Annual Reunion of Roosevelt's Rough Riders (First United States Volunteer Cavalry) veterans, including military and civilian parades, fireworks, memorial services, a tournament, musical entertainment, a grand reception, and a ball. Events are held at Duncan Opera House and "tournament grounds" in Las Vegas as well as Montezuma Hotel and Casino, Las Vegas Hot Springs.

1903: The Town of Las Vegas, west of the Gallinas River, reincorporates.

January 6, 1912: New Mexico achieves statehood.

July 1–4, 1915: The First Annual New Mexico Cowboys' Reunion, Las Vegas, New Mexico, takes place; created and sponsored by area ranchers and the Las Vegas Commercial Club.

July 3, 1915: Cowboys' Reunion Association (CRA) is established; officers and board members elected.

Appendix II

July 21, 1915: The CRA files Certificate of Incorporation with New Mexico Corporation Division as domestic profit status. Initial stock is $25,000.

1915–16: CRA purchases and refurbishes Gallinas Park and renames it Cowboys' Park.

July 4, 1916: New Mexico governor W.C. McDonald dedicates Cowboys' Park.

1917–18: The United States fights in World War I.

1924: CRA builds new Cowboys' Park one mile north of present-day Mills Avenue, Las Vegas.

1929: New York Stock Market crashes. Great Depression begins.

1931: First Phase of Cowboys' Reunion ends.

Spring 1939: Leonard Hoskins Post 24 of American Legion revives the Cowboys' Reunion, builds rodeo grounds at Legion Park, establishes new reunion dates, and creates ad hoc rodeo committee.

August 4–6, 1939: American Legion First Annual Cowboys' Reunion, sponsored by Leonard Hoskins Post 24 of American Legion, takes place.

1941–45: The United States fights in World War II.

1950–53: The United States fights in the Korean Conflict.

August 1–3, 1952: Roosevelt's Rough Riders (RRR), First United States Volunteer Cavalry Veterans, join the Cowboys' Reunion event; membership votes to hold all future RRR reunion encampments in conjunction with the Cowboys' Reunions, Las Vegas, New Mexico; special committee is established to coordinate RRR activities.

July 1–6, 1965: Cowboys' Reunion rodeo, sponsored by New Mexico Mounted Patrol Troop 3, joins with West Las Vegas Fiesta. The rodeo is held at Legion Park.

August 5–8, 1965: Travel Trailer Club of America Rally holds national convention in Las Vegas, New Mexico. RRR reunion encampment takes place August 6, Perkins Stadium, New Mexico Highlands University.

Appendix II

July 1966 and 1967: Cowboys' Reunion and Rough Rider Reunion held during "Old Town Fiesta." New Mexico Mounted Patrol Troop 3 sponsors the rodeo at Legion Park; Jesse Langdon is the sole Rough Rider in attendance.

July 4, 1968: Rough Rider Jesse Langdon makes final appearance in Las Vegas at the Old Town Fiesta parade.

August 17–19, 1984: a four-day event entitled "Ressurrection [sic] of The Cowboys' Reunion" takes place; rodeo is held at Hot Springs Boulevard.

October 23, 2009: Git Fer Vegas, Cowboy! exhibit opens at City of Las Vegas Museum and Rough Rider Memorial Collection; Mark Gardner and Rex Rideout perform the concert *Songs of the Cowboys* commemorating the work of N. Howard Thorp.

Appendix III

SELECTED ARTICLES AND POETRY

Throughout both phases of the Cowboys' Reunion, the local newspaper, the Las Vegas Daily Optic, *at times titled the* Las Vegas Optic, *and the rodeo's souvenir programs often carried supplemental and informative articles, sometimes written in the "cowboy" vernacular. These writings illustrate the changing times, attitudes, and concerns of the organizers; provide a historical context for the reunions; and, through the language, give today's readers a taste of the times.*

Las Vegas Optic, July 6, 1918
"Cowboy Show Again Proves It Is a Good Town Business Asset"

As has been the case in former years, the Cowboys Reunion of 1918 more than paid its way. Despite the handicap of inability to obtain the usual excursion rates on the railroads, despite the damper that the war was expected to cast over entertainment events, the Reunion drew as large a crowd as in any previous year. The crowd on the Fourth of July is believed to have broken all records, fully 5,250 paid admissions having been received.

Merchants state that business during the Reunion was fully up to that of former years, which means that the majority of the people who gave toward the $5,000 prize list received back in trade more than the amount of their donation.

"The business of the opening day was up to the average of the past three years," said a merchant today. "On the fourth of July we broke all records and on yesterday the trade held up to that of former years."

From a standpoint of advertising the Reunion has placed Las Vegas on the map. During the publicity campaign which preceded the show, press notices appeared in the largest publications in the country, including the big theatrical journals. Every newspaper in the state of New Mexico and many of those in Texas, Oklahoma and Kansas, especially those along the Ozark Trail, carried Reunion matter, as did several of the Denver and other Colorado papers. California papers gave the Reunion a lot of newspaper publicity on the Pacific coast. Lithographs, letters, automobile banners, handbills, and hundreds of other pieces of advertising matter went all over the west and middle west. The result was the largest attendance from a distance that the Reunion has ever enjoyed.

Beginning in 1915 with the first Reunion when Phil LeNoir conducted a spectacular and successful publicity campaign, the cowboy show has been widely advertised. The public has found that it makes good its promises, and the contestants have found it to be a square show. These things have combined to make the Reunion a drawing card. The Reunion publicity campaign was conducted this year by Colbert C. Root, secretary of the Commercial club.

There were many who were inclined to believe that it would be impossible to pull off a good show in 1918, because of war conditions. The Reunion, however, turned out to be better from the standpoint of the number and class of contestants than had been the case in former years. The attendance also was highly satisfactory. It would have been possible to have held the show over for another day, but the management prefered [*sic*] to run it through on schedule and not hold the contestants waiting the finals.

Las Vegas Optic, July 3, 1919
"Attendance Will Break Record Tomorrow"
Four Special Chair Cars Brought Crowd Here on No. 1 Today

Santa Fe train No. 1 arrived in two sections today. The first section carried four extra chair cars filled with people from Raton, Springer, Wagon Mound and other northern points coming to Las Vegas for the fourth and the Cowboys' Reunion. From all indications tomorrow will witness the largest crowd ever present at the reunion in this city.

ATTENDANCE LARGE

The attendance at the reunion yesterday [July 2, 1919] exceeded all records for a first day. The greater part of the audience was made up of people who do not live in Las Vegas. Friday is expected to see the largest crowd in town that Las Vegas has ever enjoyed entertaining. Reports from all the neighboring towns are that many people are planning to drive in this afternoon and night.

All the stores and offices will close at noon tomorrow, and Las Vegas people will attend the reunion in large numbers. The use of three gates at the grounds and the sale of tickets up town at the information booth will relieve congestion at the entrance, so that there is no likelihood of confusion and delay.

Appendix III

Las Vegas Optic, July 7, 1919
"1919 Reunion Broke Record for the Number of Visitors"

Out of town visitors were more numerous at the 1919 Cowboys Reunion than at any of its predecessors. The Commercial Club exerted every effort to find quarters for the visitors and succeeded in every instance in which its aid was asked. An information headquarters, in charge of Frank H.H. Roberts, Jr., was maintained every day and night. Over 300 people were found rooms, despite the fact that the hotels were filled, and apparently it was impossible to locate sleeping quarters after the 800 Normal [University] summer school students had been cared for. Large numbers of the visitors came in cars, bringing along their camping outfits. Had it not been for this, many people probably would have been obliged to go without accommodations.

Alvin S. Nye, secretary of the Y.M.C.A., gave the Commercial club valuable assistance by allowing cots to be place in the association gymnasium. About 25 men were given sleeping quarters in the Y on the nights of the third and fourth. On the night of July 2, 18 soldiers, members of the Seventh cavalry baseball team, slept there. Night Officers C.W. Clowes and Sam North gave valuable assistance in directing arrivals in the early hours of the morning to rooming places, lists of which were furnished by the information headquarters.

Las Vegas Daily Optic, July 31, 1947
"Etiquete [*sic*] of Rodeo in Reverse; Spectators Must Know Slang of Arena to Understand Happening"

Rodeo etiquette is something that is sort of taken for granted here in the west, but for the benefit of any tenderfoot present, a word to the wise is considered sufficient.

When the race horses round that last turn, remain quietly seated and ask the fellows seated around you not to yell, wave their fists and stand. Do this in a nice manner because the announcer will give the results shortly.

Then there is the matter of cheering the trick riders. They know you are there so why rattle them with screams and applause? You bought your ticket to see the show and all the performers are doing nicely. (Here you should comment on the weather to your neighbor as his favorite rider leaves the chute, or better, leave your seat to get a round of soft drinks for the kids. Take your time crossing in front of him.)

If he objects, remind him that this is Reunion, the time to dig out those faded levis and, despite the above advice, let your hair down for the biggest celebration of the west.

And don't duck if someone yells, "Grab that Apple." This is just friendly advice to some bronc rider who has met his match and should save his neck by grabbing the saddle horn.

Appendix III

The language of the rodeo is just as colorful as the sunset here in the west. If some of the terms are confusing, take heed. A few terms you should know:

Bicycling—The act of scratching the horse with one foot and then the other in the manner of riding a bicycle.

Biting the Dust—Thrown from a horse or steer.

Blowing a Stirrup—Losing a stirrup while riding.

Bronco—An untamed bit of horseflesh.

Bogging Time—When a rider fails to scratch his mount. Scratching—with spurs—is required in rodeo bucking events.

Broomtail—Wild mares.

Buckaroo—A bronc buster or a cowboy.

Bulldogger—Steer wrestler.

Cantle-Boarding—When a rider scratches back and braces his knees under the front part of the saddle, or cantle.

Cavy—A type of horse used in the roundup.

Chuck Wagon—Rangeland cafeteria and grocery store.

Community Loop—Slang expression to convey the idea that a roper threw an extra large loop in attempting to rope an animal—shunned by the better rodeo performers.

Critter—Man or beast.

Crow Hops—Contemptuous term for a mild bucking horse's movement.

Cut Out—Putting a steer down with his feet under him. The throw in bulldogging is not complete until the steer is flat on its side with four feet out.

Forefooting—Roping an animal by the front feet.

Grabbing the Apple—When a bronc rider grabs the saddle horn to keep from being thrown.

Gyping—Deceiving or fooling.

Hazer—Bulldogger's assistant. After the bulldogger has leaped from pony to steer[,] the hazer, mounted, picks up the former's horse and also protects him from being attacked by the steer, when the animal is released.

High Roller—A horse that seems to roll in the air when bucking.

Hobbled Stirrups—Stirrups that are tied down under the horse's belly—it is almost the same as being tied in a saddle.

Man-Killer—A vicious horse ready to strike, kick or bite at any man.

Maverick—Unbranded stray.

Outfit—Term applied to the equipment—or to the place for which a cowhand works.

Outlaw—Horse which can not be broken to ride.

Pegging—When the steer bulldogger sticks the horn of the steer in the ground. Not allowed in contests.

Pulling Leather—Holding on to the saddle when riding a bucking horse.

Appendix III

SCRATCHING—When a rider rides free on a bucking horse and moves his booted and spurred feet in a kicking motion.

SCREWING DOWN—The act of sinking spurs into the cinch while riding a bucking horse and failing to move the feet.

SEEING DAYLIGHT—When light can be seen between the rider and saddle.

SUN FISHER—Bucking horse that twists his body in the air.

TENDERFOOT—(Well, you ought to know that one).

TIGHT LEGGING—Rider fails to scratch his horse—holding legs tight against the horse.

WRANGLING—Rounding up.

That's just the beginning, for the rodeo crowd really has a language of its own.

Las Vegas Daily Optic, July 31, 1947
"Clown Has Large Task to Perform in Reunion Rodeo"
Buddy Reger and His Trick Mule to Be Present for Three Day Event

Whether he's performing with his trick mule, Rabbit, or exchanging quips with Announcer Monte Reger, spectators will think Buddy Reger, clown for the ninth annual Cowboys' Reunion, is just a funny fellow, but he plays an important part in the rodeo business.

An agile fellow who can dodge Brahmas with the speed of a bull fighter, Buddy's acts may be construed as just part of the general program, but most likely will be a maneuver to distract the attention of a Brahma from a fallen cowboy.

A rodeo clown, incidentally, is one of the highest paid performers in the dangerous game of hoofs and horns—getting paid for risking life and limb in the mist [*sic*] of kicking broncs and peeved Brahmas plus his ability to liven up any dull moments that may occur in the arena.

The first to reach a rider who has been thrown to the arena dirt, the rodeo clown is versed in the rudiments of first aid. Even though his tactics may be on the rough side, he knows what he is doing for the benefit of the rider. With a quick eye, the clown appraises possible injuries of fallen riders and knows whether it is just a case of having the wind knocked from his lungs or a more serious condition, such as broken bones.

Don't let those baggy pants and apparently slow movements fool you in the least, for the clown is a rider of ability and might even be seen riding a bucking bronc out of a chute, just for the fun of it.

"The Untold Story"
12th Annual Cowboys' Reunion Souvenir Program, August 4–6, 1950

Rodeo promotion is show business—and big business. The purses, applause, and a few of the hard knocks, go to us, and we're happy of the role our performances

Appendix III

have played in helping establish the Cowboys' Reunion as the southwest's leading rodeo.

But just as much of the success of the famed Las Vegas show is insured by the large band of boosters and volunteer workers who (often at considerable personal expense), tend to Reunion business as a year-around project. They do it as a hobby; for the satisfaction of accomplishment; and for the pride each has in his community.

For this non-participating team, there are no purses, little applause, and, tho they won't admit it, the majority of the hard knocks.

The advertisers in this book are part of the group. The official Cowboys' Reunion band is another. The service clubs and civic organizations in Las Vegas have contributed assistance too plentiful to detail completely. Ranchers and stockmen, the Mounted Patrol, Sheriff's Posse, the Mounted Square Dance Club, all have been unselfish in cooperation. Housewives, eager to boost the event, were among the many who mailed out Reunion Booster postal cards. And this is the time of the year that youngsters of Las Vegas forget about hoping to be aviators when they grow up, and set sights on one of the finest lifes [sic] of all—the cowboy's.

Credit also must go to Highlands University, to the many participants in the opening parade, and to the hundreds who did their part by wearing western togs during the week preceding the show. The Civil Air Patrol dropped thousands of advertising leaflets on surrounding communities, as well as arranging for the "breakfast flight" for southwest pilots on Sunday, Aug. 6.

In keeping with its role as a constant advertiser for the community, the Las Vegas–San Miguel Chamber of Commerce has rallied behind the Cowboys' Reunion association.

These thousands of fans who fill the arena's seats contributed their part. It even seems the livestock has been infected with that spirit which has made the Cowboys' Reunion famous—the calves appear more frisky, the broncs buck harder, and the steers are a bit more rugged.

Special recognition, we feel, should go to those who, at expense of other interests, worked daily, for long months, on the show's promotion. This was the group that you saw each Friday night in executive meetings at the Castañeda Hotel. A bronc rider may have his discomforts, but this group gets the headaches—and we give them a few ourselves.

You'll find the names of the major committees in charge of the rodeo elsewhere in the program. You may thank them, but we wish to thank all of you for your help in making this show more than just another rodeo—for making it the Cowboys' Reunion.

Appendix III

Las Vegas Daily Optic, August 6, 1953
"Introduction of Brahmas Boosted Excitement on Rodeoing Arenas"

About 20 years ago [circa 1933] somebody thought it would be a rodeo stimulant if Brahmas, the sacred cattle of India, were used in the bull riding event. Huge, colorful, and exotic, they turned out to be a natural for rodeo. They were fierce and truculent, giving the paying spectator a real thrill.

Today Brahma bull riding, a "must" on every progressive rodeo's program, is an event that would prostrate the Indian breeders of the world's oldest cattle. Far from being idolized, the rodeo Brahma bull is the bellowing recipient of threats, curses, and clods of dirt, all hurled with deadly earnestness by cowboys who make a living trying to stay on its mammoth hide for eight seconds.

Yes, only eight tiny seconds. But when a cowboy's about to leave the back of a "spinner," a twisting bull that turns in tight circles, those seconds stretch themselves out. Of all the different types of buckers. The spinning bull is the most dangerous and most feared. After a rider hits the dirt, a spinning bull often whirls into him, hooking with its heavy horns. Other bulls buck straight away, twist in different directions, or lunge high in the air. But for their size—some weigh up to a ton—they are amazingly coordinated and graceful, and some can clear six-foot fences in a single, swooping bound.

In rodeo it's the bad bull that's the good one. Rodeo producers and stock contractors are always on the lookout for odd, off-colored, spectacular Brahmas to add gusto to their rodeo string.

However, it's possible to make these humped creatures too tough. Once a truly bad one turns into a killer, that bull is on the "useless" list. In the chute, these deceptively gentle-eyed, floppy-eared animals stand quietly—but when the gate flies open they throw a "whingding."

One of the best bucking bulls in the business—a spinner—was owned by Otho Kinsley, a rodeo stock contractor from Amando, Ariz. Speck, so named because of its mottled coloring, bucked off some of the top boys. The bull was finally conquered by Dick Griffin of Scottsdale, Ariz., in 1946, in a ride which produced a bet of $1,000 on each side.

Kinsley maintains these strange animals have two natures. Passive and quiet out on pasture, they can become raging monsters when confined. Silver City, N.M. will always remember one chaotic rodeo when Kinsley's bulls broke out of the catch pens[,] smashed the grandstands, and stampeded hundreds of hysterical spectators. These were the same bulls Kinsley could approach on foot while they grazed at his ranch a few days before.

One of the main attractions of bull riding is the antics the riders and the rodeo clowns go through in avoiding the sharp hoofs and horns of the Brahmas. The clown is a life-saver and must be extremely fleet to keep ahead of a charging bull. It's the clown's job to protect a fallen rider from a bull. In doing so, he takes great risks, much to the delight of the crowd, and seems to care little for his own welfare. This sort of play, reminiscent of the Roman Coliseum spectacles where man was pitted against ferocious animals, has held audience's attention for centuries. It's still doing it in rodeo.

Las Vegas Daily Optic, July 1, 1965
"A Cowboy's Dream of Heaven" by Oscar Ford

(Dedicated to the spiritual side of cowboy life, that the average town folk or city dweller fails to comprehend.)

There's a land beyond the river
Where the grass is always green:
Where the wild roses bloom eternal
With fragrance to please a queen:
Where each day is filled with sunshine,
Where the nights are nice and cool,
Where all the people are good neighbors
And live by the Golden Rule.

There's a land beyond the river
Where the weather is so calm and still:
Where all may drink of cold spring water
As it comes trickling down the hill:
Where one can hear the droll humming
Of the lazy bumble bee,
And see a pair of little sparrows
Nesting high in yonder tree.

There's a land beyond the river
That's known to us as a glory land:
Where all the buildings were erected
By one gesture of God's hand:
Where all are bedecked with jewels
That are truly rich and rare.
And children romping with the angels
Up and down the golden stair.

There's a land beyond the river
Where all of us would like to go:
Where we can live in peace forever
With no more wild oats to sow:
But we must plan for some correction
So on that final round-up day
Each cowboy may pass inspection
And then move there to stay.

Appendix IV

Cowhands and Rough Riders

What's the Connection?

"Git Fer Vegas, Cowboy!" was the cry all over New Mexico in 1915 when the First Annual Cowboys' Reunion took to the streets of Las Vegas. There was not a Rough Rider in sight. Roosevelt's Rough Riders had held one reunion encampment in Las Vegas, New Mexico, in June 1899. Yet local history and lore linked these two reunions in both the popular media and historical narratives. An examination of the reunions and their timing and purposes may illuminate this tenuous and possibly artificial relationship.

The soldiers of the First United States Volunteer Cavalry, dubbed Roosevelt's Rough Riders by the press of their time, were mustered out in the fall of 1898 after sharing service in Cuba. On June 24, 25 and 26, 1899, those veterans reunited in Las Vegas, New Mexico. They chose the June dates to commemorate the Battle of Las Guasimas, Cuba, in which they fought and some of their number died. Having been recruited from the Southwest because of their fearlessness and riding abilities, most of the veterans were by profession cowhands, ranchmen, or lawmen, and several had performed with Buffalo Bill's Wild West Show. They made this first reunion an encampment, and they set up tents and mess facilities in Lincoln Park, Las Vegas.

The official program for that first reunion included meetings, a memorial service, regimental and equine reviews, parades, receptions, dances, a pyrotechnic display, a performance of "The Creation," an oration by Josef Hayden, by the Las Vegas Oratorio Society, and a "Tournament." The three-day tournament involved various types of athletic games and several rodeo events—a lassoing contest, calf roping, bronc riding, and a potato race. The activities associated with the first Rough Rider Encampment were similar to those of the Cowboys' Reunion conceived of and executed sixteen years later.

Appendix IV

The Rough Riders established their own organization, Roosevelt's Rough Rider Association (RRR), set the dates of their annual encampments as June 24–26, and determined to meet in various locations throughout the country. In 1949, the Rough Riders returned to Las Vegas to celebrate their Golden Jubilee. In 1948, they had been invited to hold their fiftieth anniversary reunion in Las Vegas at the Cowboys' Reunion. However, that suggestion met with some resistance. In a letter to William J. Love, Roger S. Fitch (though he agreed that Las Vegas was an excellent site for the jubilee) stated that "there would not be many of us attending the reunion if it were held at any time other than the historic June 24," and he made it clear that he would not support the Rough Riders Reunion being "held in conjunction with or simultaneously with a cowboy's reunion." By 1952, things had changed. The RRR membership met in Las Vegas during the Cowboys' Reunion and voted to meet annually during each Cowboys' Reunion event until the "last man" could not attend.

In the spring of 1915, Las Vegas area ranchers and cowboys collaborated with the Las Vegas Commercial Club, a Greater Las Vegas booster association, and put on the First Annual New Mexico Cowboys' Reunion, July 1–4. On July 3, due to the success of the initial reunion, the organizers incorporated as the Cowboys' Reunion Association (CRA) for the express purpose of ensuring that the event would occur annually. In addition, the CRA stipulated that the "cowboys at large" would both "own and control the affairs at all times." The CRA Cowboys' Reunion took place annually until 1931 and was exclusively a cowhand-rancher affair. In 1939, Leonard Hoskins Post No. 24 of the American Legion revived the Cowboys' Reunion event, which continued, with some changes in sponsorship, until 1967.

Looking back through the nearly forty-six-year Cowboys' Reunion span, the connection with the Rough Riders was fifteen years (1952–67), about one-third of the history of the Cowboys' Reunion. However, in the hearts and minds of Las Vegans, several variables came together to meld these two reunions. First was the consistent publicity asserting that the roots of the Cowboys' Reunion lay in the rodeo events of the First Rough Riders Reunion. Second are the memories of community members who experienced the Rough Riders and Cowboys' Reunion rodeos from 1952 to 1967. Third is the terminology.

The terms get easily confused. Rodeo and working cowhands are, after all, rough riders. The members of the Rough Riders came from the ranks of working cowhands, one difference being that, unlike the Cowboys' Reunions, there were no female Rough Riders. A reunion is a reunion is an encampment. Finally, from 1952 to 1967, when the Rough Riders came to town, they came as part of the Rough Riders and Cowboys' Reunion, sometimes shortened to the Rough Riders Reunion—after all, a rider is a rider is a rough rider.

Today, almost one hundred years since the first Cowboys' Reunion, a few descendants of the original CRA members recall that first phase through the recollections of parents and grandparents; however, most Las Vegans attended the American Legion phase of the Cowboys' Reunion and saw the Rough Riders dashing into the rodeo arena on horseback among the cowboys. Many Las Vegans were present when the veterans read their memoirs and reminisced. To those young spectators, the Rough Riders were an integral part of the Cowboys' Reunion. After all, they were "re-unionizing," too, but as veterans of the Spanish-American War.

Ultimately, it was the repeated focus of the publicity surrounding the annual Cowboys' Reunion that cemented the tenuous relationship between the two. This connection was a double-edged sword: on the one hand, it provided the Cowboys' Reunion an undeniable draw by connecting it to the Roosevelt's Rough Riders Reunion; on the other hand, it forever confused the two events and their disparate origins and motivations. Furthermore, this publicity-driven connection found its way into various historical narratives.

Some examples of the publicity hooplas include catchphrases in souvenir programs and advertisements. In 1949, perhaps because the Rough Riders held their Golden Jubilee Anniversary in June at Las Vegas, the Cowboys' Reunion literature in August included statements noting that the Cowboys' Reunion is "the offspring of the Rough Riders Reunion" and the show that Theodore Roosevelt started. In a 1949 article in *New Mexico Magazine*, Paul E. Cunningham wrote, "The men who drove twice their number before them as they charged up San Juan Hill danced, reminisced, and attended the first Cowboys' Reunion ever staged in Las Vegas. Since that time the rodeo has become an annual event." By the following year, the connection was unquestioned. The 1950 Cowboys' Reunion rodeo program was subtitled "The Show that Teddy Roosevelt Started" and included a photograph of Roosevelt, with a caption reading, "Col. Theodore Roosevelt, whose Rough Riders Reunion of 1899 in Las Vegas set a precedent for the Cowboys' Reunion." Perhaps to the members of the CRA the 1899 reunion had set a precedent, but the documentation notes otherwise; it is more likely that they were following precedents set by Cheyenne, Wyoming, and Pendleton, Oregon.

Historical texts, both of and about the period, often perpetuate the connection between the Rough Riders encampments and the Cowboys' Reunions. Perrigo, in *Las Vegas and the Rough Riders*, proposes that the "performance [of rodeo events in 1899] was a forerunner of the modern rodeo" when, in fact, it was a reflection of the times and the interests of the veterans. In Lesley Poling Kempes's account of the Harvey Girls in Las Vegas, the narrative includes a description of the Rough Riders Reunion and indicates in the years following the 1899 encampment that "the annual event became known as the Rough Riders and Cowboys Reunion...until its discontinuance in 1948." As we have seen, the Rough Riders and Cowboys' Reunion did not come into being until 1952 and was not discontinued until

Appendix IV

1967. Many sources, both primary and secondary, provided researchers and historians with confusing and, at times, erroneous data.

One of many newspaper accounts of the late 1940s provides a brief but fictitious history: "This is the ninth annual Cowboys' Reunion as sponsored by Leonard Hoskins Post 24, American Legion, but it is a throwback to 1889 [sic] when Teddy Roosevelt's Rough Riders staged the first Reunion in Las Vegas. Then after a brief lapse, the Reunion was changed to Cowboys' Reunion and initial showing was in 1915."

If the Cowboys' Reunion harkened back to a prior history beyond the regional and ranch rodeos of the late nineteenth century, it would have been to the very old tradition of "rodeo," the spontaneous cowhand gatherings at the end of a long drive in all cultures and peoples who raised herd animals. Furthermore, even discounting the error, 1889 for 1899, the "brief lapse" represents sixteen years, almost a generation.

One of the more accurate, as well as colorful, stories of the Cowboys' Reunion is that of S. Omar Barker in his "recollections of rodeo in New Mexico" in the article "Git Fer Vegas, Cowboy!" from the *Frontier Times* journal. Barker recounted a history of the Cowboys' Reunion beginning with the founding members of the CRA and Phil LeNoir of the Commercial Club. As Barker summed it up:

> *My own recollections of rodeo in New Mexico center around the old Las Vegas Cowboys' Reunion, first staged on July 4, 1915. It was a ripsnorting contest and a real ranch-folks Reunion with more camper-outers than hotel-stoppers in town. All, or nearly all, the contestants were working cowboys from New Mexico ranches. The Reunion was unique among rodeos in that only cattle-owning ranchmen could serve on its eleven-man board of directors.*

The Las Vegas Cowboys' Reunion and its rodeo were conceived of and produced by Las Vegas area ranchers and working cowhands. Although it evolved alongside rodeo and for a time flirted with professional status, the reunion rodeo primarily remained outside the Professional Rodeo Association boundaries. From 1952 to 1967, the Cowboys' Reunion was proud to partner up with Roosevelt's Rough Riders. The partnership sustained both groups and brought increased national attention to the community and its ranching heritage. But neither organization spawned the other. They shared the common ground of "get-togetherness" and equine sport, and both groups, separately and together, enjoyed "a ripsnorting contest."

Sources

Vital to telling this history of the Las Vegas Cowboys' Reunion are the various and numerous sources of information. Fortunately, many of these sources, mostly primary, are preserved and held within the city. The sources of direct quotations are identified within the text. Below is a listing of all resources, both primary and secondary, that were cited or consulted. Much valuable information and anecdotes came from informal discussions with people who had participated in or attended the Cowboys' Reunions.

Books and Articles

Barker, S. Omar. "Git Fer Vegas, Cowboy!" *Frontier Times* 41 (December–January 1968): 20–21, 59–62.

———. "Reunion at Las Vegas." *New Mexico Magazine* 36, no. 6 (June 1958): 24–25, 53.

Cabeza de Baca, Fabiola. *We Fed Them Cactus.* Albuquerque: University of New Mexico Press, 1954.

Callon, Milton W. *Las Vegas, New Mexico…The Town that Wouldn't Gamble.* Las Vegas, NM: Las Vegas Publishing Company, 1962.

Crandall, Judy. *Cowgirls: Early Images and Collectibles.* Atglen, PA: Schiffer Publishing, 1994.

Cunningham, Paul E. "Rough Riders' Reunion." *New Mexico Magazine* (June 1949): 22.

Dingus, Charles. "Reunion Days." *New Mexico Magazine* 19, no. 8 (August 1941): 14–15, 47.

Dobson, G.B. "Frontier Days." Wyoming Tales and Trails, Featuring Photographs and History of Old Wyoming. www.wyomingtalesandtrails.com.

Sources

Everett, Dianna. "Beutler Brothers." Oklahoma Historical Society's Encyclopedia of Oklahoma History & Culture. http://digital.library.okstate.edu/encyclopedia/entries/B/BE029.html.

Fredriksson, Kristine. *American Rodeo from Buffalo Bill to Big Business.* College Station: Texas A&M University Press, 1985.

Jordan, Teresa. *Cowgirls: Women of the West.* Lincoln: University of Nebraska Press, 1982.

New Mexico Business Directory. Denver, CO: Gazetteer Publishing Company, 1903–4, 1915, 1928.

New Mexico: The Land of Opportunity—Official Data on the Resources and Industries of New Mexico—The Sunshine State. Albuquerque, NM: Press of the Albuquerque Morning Journal, 1915.

Perrigo, Lynn I. *Gateway to Glorieta. A History of Las Vegas, New Mexico.* Boulder, CO: Pruett Publishing Company, 1982. Facsimile reprint, Santa Fe, NM: Sunstone Press, 2010.

———. *Las Vegas and the Rough Riders.* Las Vegas, NM: Museum Board of the City of Las Vegas Museum, 1961.

Poling-Kempes, Lesley. *The Harvey Girls.* New York: Paragon House, 1991.

"The Rough Riders Ride Again." *Life* 33, no. 8 (August 25, 1952): 43–45.

Rudisill, Richard. *Photographers of the New Mexico Territory 1854–1912.* Santa Fe: Museum of New Mexico Press, 1973.

Slatta, Richard W. *The Cowboy Encyclopedia.* New York: W.W. Norton & Company, 1994.

Teatime with the Old-Timers. Compact Disc. Baca Broadcasting LLC, KFUN-AM 1230, J.P. Baca. August 1, 2006, 5:00 p.m. to 6:30 p.m., CCHP#A1.

Thorp, N. Howard. *Songs of the Cowboys.* Lincoln: University of Nebraska Press, 1921.

Vivian, Walter. "Return of the Rough Riders." *New Mexico Magazine* (June 1953): 13–15, 37.

Walker, Dale L. "The Next to the Last Man: Rough Rider Frank Brito." *Nova* (February–April 1971).

Ward, W.G., Robert J. Taupert and R.E. Twitchell, eds. *Las Vegas Gallinas Park and the Scenic Highway.* Las Vegas, NM: Optic Company, 1904.

The Wild Bunch 1, no. 10 (January [1916]); 1, no. 11 (February 1916); and 2, no. 2 (June 1916).

Archives

Citizens Committee for Historic Preservation, Las Vegas, New Mexico.

City of Las Vegas Museum and Rough Rider Memorial Collection, Las Vegas, New Mexico.

Sources

New Mexico Highlands University Donnelly Library, Las Vegas, New Mexico.
Palace of the Governors Photo Archives, Santa Fe, New Mexico.

Private Collections

Elsie Tapia Collection, Las Vegas, New Mexico.
George M. "Dogie" Jones Collection, Watrous, New Mexico.

Newspapers

Albuquerque Evening Herald
Las Vegas Daily Optic
National Tribune—The Stars and Stripes, Washington, D.C.

INDEX

A

Abbett, Robert K. 64, 100
Allen, Prairie Lillie 49
Allen, Slim 42, 44
Allingham, Bernie 95
Al Thrasher and His Orchestra 64, 102
American Legion 21, 23, 57, 58, 59, 60, 63, 64, 65, 68, 71, 72, 76, 79, 80, 81, 84, 92
American Legion Leonard Hoskins Post No. 24 21, 57, 87
American Legion Rodeo Arena 59, 60, 79
Annie, Texas 27, 33, 44, 49, 101
Armijo, Judge 54
Arrott, James W. 73, 74, 75, 76, 79, 80
Atchison, Topeka & Santa Fe Railway (AT&SF) 13, 14, 29
  Hot Springs Branch 29
Atkinson, Fred 47
Atkinson, J.O. 59
Atkinson, Joe 60
Augur, Ruth Monro 22, 42, 51
Austin, J.V. "Tex" 22, 27, 35, 38, 50, 53
Autry, Gene 65

B

Bagley, A.B. 35
Bagley, Brite 29
Barker, Omar S. 23, 29, 43, 44, 53, 54, 63
Baumann, John 19
Belle, Montana 22, 47, 49
Beutler brothers 21, 70, 76, 81
  Elra 70
  Jake 70
  Lynn 70
Bibb, Dee 53, 62, 63, 76
Bills, Dick 79
Blood, Mayor 42
Borein, Edward 23, 45, 51, 64
Bozeman, Pascal 53
Brahma bulls 59, 67, 70
Briggs, Texas George 49
Brito, Frank C. 85
Buffalo Bill's Wild West Show 19
Burns, Audrey 53

C

Calgary Exhibition and Stampede 20
Callon, Milton W. 33, 54
Campbell, Glen 80
Camp Luna 65
Cassidy, Gerald 51

INDEX

Castañeda Hotel 64, 76, 80, 83, 87, 112
Cheyenne Frontier Days 20, 30, 71, 75
Chief (horse) 49
Citizens Bank of Clovis 94
City of Las Vegas 14, 85
City of Las Vegas Museum and Rough Rider Memorial Collection 85, 86, 93, 94
Civil Air Patrol 72
Clancy, Frederick "Foghorn" 29, 37, 49
Clayton Troubadours 80
Clovis Carver Public Library 94
Clowes, C.W. 109
Cody, William F. "Buffalo Bill" 19
Commercial Club 25, 26
Connery, Ed 60
Cowboys' Band. *See* Las Vegas Cowboys' Reunion Band
Cowboys' Park 38, 42, 53
Cowboys' Reunion and Rodeo Association 71, 74, 83
Cowboys' Reunion Association 14, 26, 27, 34, 36, 50, 60, 62, 71, 75, 83
Cowboys' Reunion Band. *See* Las Vegas Cowboys' Reunion Band
Cowboys' Reunion resurrection 87
Cowboys' Turtle Association 59
Cowgirls 65
"Creation, The" 115
Creative Printers Inc. 87
Crimmins, Colonel Martin 74, 75
Cunningham, Paul E. 117

D

Davey, Randall 22, 51
Davis, M.J. 23, 64
Dead Horse Ranch 78
Denny, Robert W. 73, 74
Des Marais, Dr. M.F. 27
Dick Bills & the Sandia Mountain Boys 79
Dillon, Governor 54
Dingus, Charles 60, 62, 64

Dukeminier, Ray 67
Duncan Opera House 30, 53, 103

E

Eckerd, "Powder Face" 47
Eisenhower, President Dwight D. 80
Elks Lodge 81
Elton Travis Band 80
Everett, Dianna 70

F

Fenton, Grahame 82
First United States Volunteer Cavalry 22, 74, 80
Fleming, George A. 26
Fort Union 13, 14, 76
Fredriksson, Kristine 17, 18, 19, 21, 58, 59, 65, 71
French, James A. 30
Friends of the City of Las Vegas Museum 94

G

Gallegos, Ed 44
Gallinas Park 27, 29, 30, 38, 42, 87
Gallinas River 13, 22, 27, 29, 36
Gardner, Mark 94
Garrett, Sammy 49
Gortner, Mrs. W.E. 27
Grand Army of the Republic (GAR) 44
Great Depression 21, 87, 104
Greater Las Vegas, New Mexico, Fiesta Committee 84, 87

H

Hainlen Studio 64
Heastonaires, the 65, 80
Henderson, Prairie Rose (Ann Robbins) 22, 49
Highlands University 72
Hines, Tommy 80
Hispano Chamber of Commerce 87

Index

Hoffman & Graubarth 67
Hurley, Patrick 79
Huyck, E.E. 35

J

James, Will 23
Jaycees 81
Joe's Ringside Inn 64
Jones, George M. "Butch" 35, 83
Jones, George M. "Dogie" 83
Jones, H.L. 64
Jordan, Teresa 47, 65
Jr. Jaycees 87
Judd, Johnny 27, 49, 54

K

Kansas City Slide Company 43
Kasper's Band 53
Keenan, M.G. 35
Kew, George 76
Kiwanis Club 81
Knight, Jack 54, 57, 60

L

Langdon, Jesse 74, 76, 84, 85
Las Guasimas 72, 80, 115
Las Vegas–San Miguel Chamber of Commerce 72, 112
Las Vegas Armory 36, 54, 65, 84
Las Vegas Cowboys' Reunion Band 21, 53
Las Vegas Driving Park and Fair Association 29
Las Vegas Electric Trolley 29
Las Vegas Lions Club 64
Las Vegas Oratorio Society 115
Las Vegas Twirlers 77
Lee Company 67
Legion Park Rodeo Grounds 60, 68, 87
LeNoir, Phil 36, 37, 43, 44, 45, 50, 53, 56
Leonard Hoskins Post No. 24. *See* American Legion Leonard Hoskins Post No. 24

Levi Strauss 67
Lewis, C.C. 30
Lewis, Hayward 30
Life magazine 76
Lindsey, Clyde 49, 65
Los Alamos National Laboratory Foundation 94
Los Nativos 64
Love, William 85
Lutz, Ruth 80
Lynam, Walter 30, 35

M

Madison Square Garden Rodeo 60, 78
McBee, Blanche 67
McBee, Lloyd 67
McDonald, W.C. 38, 42
McGinty, Billy 74, 76
Meadow City 50
Meadows Hotel 64
Melodylanders, the 54
Mix, Tom 22, 25, 27, 33
Montezuma Club 26
Mounted Square Dance Club 72, 112
Mullins, Johnny 21, 59

N

National Finals Rodeo Commission 83
Naylor, Walter A. 27, 34, 35
Neafus, J.O. 35
Ned and His Melody Busters 64
Newman, Almeron 43
New Mexico Humanities Council 94
New Mexico Magazine 53, 60, 78, 117
New Mexico Mounted Patrol Troop 3 84, 92
New York Stock Market 21, 55
Normal University 109
Norris, Frank C. 84
Nye, Alvin S. 109

O

O'Malley, Charles 33, 45, 80
Oates, Marie 84

125

INDEX

Old Town Fiesta 83, 84, 85
Old Town Plaza Park 27, 84
120 Engineers' Band 102
Ozark Trail 107

P

Panama-California Exposition 26
Pawnee Bill's Wild West 19
Pearson, W.B. "Idaho Bill" 22, 27, 50
Pendleton Round Up 20
Perrigo, Lynn I. 13, 15, 25, 29, 42, 54, 86, 117

Q

Queen for a Day 23, 80

R

Ray, Jack 49
Red, Bugger 47
Reger, Buddy 71
Reger, Virginia 65, 70
Reichelderfer, Harry 80
Ressurrection of the Cowboys' Reunion, The 87
Reunion News 42, 43, 44, 45, 54
Rex Studio 64
Rideout, Rex 94
Roberts, Frank H.H. 109
Roberts, Frank S. 82
Roberts, Mrs. Frank H.H. 27
Romero, Mayor M.A. 59
Romero, Secundino 35
Roosevelt, Theodore 72, 75, 76
Roosevelt's Rough Rider Association 22, 72, 75, 77, 116
Root, Colbert C. 27, 108
Rose, Prairie 47
Rotary Club 81
Rough Riders 23, 25, 26, 72, 74, 75, 76, 77, 79, 80, 82, 84, 85, 86, 92
Rough Riders Museum 87
Rude, Ike 71
Rumans, Walter 47

S

Salmon, Petey 77
Sandefer, Diana 76
Sandefer, Gib 79
Sangre de Cristo Mountains 13
San Miguel County 14, 15, 26, 47, 57
Santa Fe Trail 13, 14
Sapello Rough Riders Rodeo Association 87
Scheihagen, W.R. "Shy" 82, 84, 85
Schiele, Louis F. 74
Selig Motion Picture Company's Daredevil Performers 33
Selig Polyscope Copmany 27
Sena, Apolonio A. 35
7 Notes, the 65, 102
Sheriff's Posse 72, 112
Shoulder, Jim 23
Simison Orchestra 54
Smith, Mayor H.M. 27
Songs of the Cowboys 50, 94
Songs of the Cowboys Centennial Concert 94
Sore in the Saddle 64
Spanish-American War 22, 76, 117
Springer, William H. 34, 35
Stacel, Ben 47
Stanton, Bill 44, 45, 47
Steiner, Tommy 21, 76
Steiner Rodeo Company 76, 81
Stewart, Donald 35
Stokes, L.L. "Boone" 82, 83, 86
Stroud, Leonard 44, 49
Stroud, Mayme 44, 49, 65
Sutherland, George 30

T

Tapia, Dolores 95
Tapia, Ernesto 67
Taupert, Robert 29
"Teatime with the Old-Timers" 77, 80
Thatcher, Gordy Maxine 80
Thompson, H.C. 64
Thorp, N. Howard "Jack" 22, 50, 94
Todhunter, Ozella 82, 85